**FOREWORD BY DR. HOWARD ADAMS**

# Guaranteed 4.0

**Follow our 3-step plan and if
you DON'T make all A's,
we will GIVE YOU
$100!**

## Donna O. Johnson & Y.C. Chen

**A simple 3-step brain-based learning system
to help students learn how to learn!**

Cover: Alpha Advertising (www.alphaadvertising.com)
Layout: Pine Hill Graphics (www.pinehillgraphics.com)
Illustration: Multimedia Street (www.multimediastreet.com)

Published by:
JCYC Studio
Dallas, Texas
www.JCYCStudio.com

*In Cooperation with*
Guaranteed 4.0 Learning System, LLC
*17194 Preston Road, Suite 102*
*Mail Code 338*
*Dallas, TX 75248*
*www.Guaranteed4.com*

Cover Design by Alpha Advertising
Interior Design by Pine Hill Graphics

Packaged by Pine Hill Graphics

Library of Congress Cataloging-in-Publication Data
*(Provided by Cassidy Cataloguing Services, Inc.)*

Johnson, Donna O.

   Guaranteed 4.0 : simple 3-step brain-based learning strategies to help
   students learn how to learn! / Donna O. Johnson & Y. C. Chen. -- 1st ed.
   -- Dallas, TX : JCYC Studio, 2004.

      p. ; cm.

      ISBN: 0-9742648-0-6

      1. Study skills. 2. Learning. 3. Academic achievement. I. Chen, Y.
   C. II. Title.

LB1049 .J64 2004

371.3/028/1--dc22                            0403

# Table of Contents

✦ ✦ ✦ ✦ ✦ ✦ ✦ ✦ ✦ ✦ ✦ ✦ ✦ ✦ ✦ ✦ ✦

Foreword. . . . . . . . . . . . . . . . . . . . . . . . . . . . . . . . . . . . . . . . . . . . . . 5
Acknowledgments . . . . . . . . . . . . . . . . . . . . . . . . . . . . . . . . . . . . . 7
Introduction . . . . . . . . . . . . . . . . . . . . . . . . . . . . . . . . . . . . . . . . . 11
Our $100 Guarantee & Success Stories . . . . . . . . . . . . . . . . . . 13
Tips to get the most out of this book . . . . . . . . . . . . . . . . . . . . 17

## Part I: Donna O.'s Guaranteed 4.0 Plan . . . . . . . . . . . . . 19

### Chapter I: Stress Management. . . . . . . . . . . . . . . . . . . . . . . . . 21
*What is stress?*
*Is stress normal?*
*How can I manage stress?*
*Chapter I Review*

### Chapter II: Time Management. . . . . . . . . . . . . . . . . . . . . . . . . 27
*WHAT to do vs. HOW to do it*
*What do college students do with their time every week?*
*Time analysis table*
*Guaranteed 4.0 time management principles*
*Chapter II Review*

### Chapter III: Guaranteed 3 steps to a 4.0 GPA . . . . . . . . . . . . . . 39
*Step 1. Unwritten Rules of the Classroom . . . . . . . . . . . . . . 39*
   Why & Where
   The Unwritten Rules
   Step 1 Review

*Step 2. Secrets & Insights about Your Professor. . . . . . . . . . 49*
   POH- Why & When
   3 Secrets About Your Professors
      (that every student should know!)
   Step 2 Review

*Step 3. A Proven Method for Academic Success . . . . . . . . . 57*
*What are you supposed to do before going to class?*
   Bullet Point Reading (BPR) - Read to Remember!
   A Guaranteed 4.0 Principle
   Examples of BPR
   Section Summary - I

*Classroom Behavior Demystified*
    What should I do with my class notes?
    Bullet Point Notes (BPN) - How & When
    Help! I procrastinate!
    Section Summary - II

*Understanding the Principles with Bullet Point Concepts (BPC)*
    Importance of BPC
    Examples of BPC
    True Story about SOAP BPC
    A SECRET weapon to stay on top of it all—Bullet Point Notebook
    Section Summary - III

*3 Things about the Word "Study"*
    Section Summary - IV

**Chapter IV: Final Declaration** . . . . . . . . . . . . . . . . . . . . . . . . . . . . .91
    *No more study!*
    *Donna O.'s 5 Questions of Life*

**Part 2: Applying the 4.0 Plan—A Student's Perspective . . . 95**

    **Introduction to Part 2** . . . . . . . . . . . . . . . . . . . . . . . . . . . . . . . . . . 97

    **Frequently Asked Questions** . . . . . . . . . . . . . . . . . . . . . . . . . . . . . 99

**Appendix: Blank Charts and Examples.** . . . . . . . . . . . . . 131

# Foreword

✦ ✦ ✦ ✦ ✦ ✦ ✦ ✦ ✦ ✦ ✦ ✦ ✦ ✦ ✦ ✦

By Dr. Howard Adams

I have maintained for a long time that people look outside themselves to find out what they must do to be successful. Students are constantly in search of a success "magic potion" or "hidden secret." However, I believe that success begins with YOU—the person who is reading this book.

This book is designed specifically to aid in navigating the process and potential challenges of higher education. It addresses tangible and intangible obstacles students may encounter in their pursuit of academic excellence. However, this is more than just another study skills book. The Guaranteed 4.0 Learning System empowers students to learn on a fundamental level; a life-long skill for success that can have many applications.

I often define mentoring as "a relationship between individuals for mutual learning and influence." From Donna O.'s involvement with the National Society of Black Engineers (NSBE) as the National Chairperson, as an engineer at Amoco and to her efforts as the Founder and President of the Guaranteed 4.0 Learning System, I have witnessed her unwavering commitment for academic excellence as her mentor. On a personal note, her passion for student performance and self-efficacy has been a point of mutual learning and respect.

The Guaranteed 4.0 Seminars have helped countless students—from 6th graders to PhD candidates. (One of my doctoral students had an amazing transformation after putting the plan into action.) While Donna O. and her staff present similar information in a seminar format, it is really a pleasure to see this book being published so many more students can reap the benefits from this proven system.

# Acknowledgments

◆ ◆ ◆ ◆ ◆ ◆ ◆ ◆ ◆ ◆ ◆ ◆ ◆ ◆ ◆ ◆ ◆

## Donna O. Johnson

**My first acknowledgement could only go to God.** Thank you for your continuously passionate love and for trusting me with 4.0's mission of being a light in the midst of darkness. It is only by your grace that this book exists. I pray that it blesses all who read it!

**I would also like to acknowledge my family.** If it were possible to choose your own family, I would choose my God given family again and again. Many thanks to:

- My grandmother, Pearle Greer Richards, for making school a fun game on her front porch and giving me a fundamental love for learning
- My mother, for being my example of God's unconditional love and my hero and for making me believe that I could do anything
- Aunt Minnie & Uncle Chick, my second mother & father, for always supporting me and making my summers fun and productive
- My big sister, Marika, for being my strength every time I really needed her
- My oldest brother, Keith, for being my example of diligence and discipline
- Vernon, my "twin brother", for being my best friend from birth and always my advocate
- Michael, my beloved, for being wise, patient, and wonderful and teaching me new dimensions of God's love
- My "play brother", Kevin, for his support and commitment
- And my aunts, uncles, cousins, in-laws, nephews, nieces, and Godsons.

**I would like to express my appreciation to the following people who have significantly impacted my personal development:**

- My Spiritual parents & Godparents: Mr. & Mrs. Alton Fleming, Drs. Chester & Vonda Pipkin, Bishop & Mrs. Henry M. Williamson, Sr., Mr. & Mrs. Joe McNeally, Sr., Rev. & Mrs. K. C. Phillips, Marieta Julean, Apostle Napoleon Williams, Nell Christopher, Mr. & Mrs. Perry Sampson, and Drs. Robert & Carolyn Smith
- My Mentors: Councilwoman Barbara Swearengen Holt, Betty Crawford, Pastor Dan Dorthalina, Derrick Scott, Don Wilson, Dwight Jackson, Apostle Francis Myles, Gene Washington, Gwen Packnett, Dr. Howard Adams, Dr. Kaye Jeter, Marion Blalock, Dr. Richard Price, Sadie Swyne and Apostle Stephen Mwanaliti
- UT-College of Engineering and my wonderful classmates who supported me through the trial and error of college academics: Carolyn Benton, Craig Cassel, Charles Perkins, David Jones, Debra Robinson, Ed Davis, James Smith, Rodney Johnson, Sonia Martinez, Terry Ramos, Tom Backus, and Dr. Irvin Osborne-Lee.
- The community of Center, Texas

**I would like to acknowledge the National Society of Black Engineers where Guaranteed 4.0 was first presented and some of my colleagues there:**

Charles Walker, Chris Davis, David Fleming, Dr. David Porter, Dr. Gary May, Karl Reid, Dr. Karen Butler-Purry, LaRence Snowden, Louis Hurston, Michelle Lezama, Drs. Norman & Janet Fortenberry, Richard White, Troy & Sonya Stovall, Virginia Booth, the Region V Advisory Board, and the National Advisory Board.

Over the years, many colleagues have been instrumental in 4.0's business development. Some of them are:

Aileen Walter, Angela Knight, Anthea Jones, Ava Youngblood, Betty Chavis, Mr. & Mrs. Carl Vaughan, Charles Walton, Cheryl Cambridge, Dr. Cheryl Washington, Dr. Cynthia McIntyre, Debbie McClean, Dundee Holt, Erica Cain, Gabe Najera, Dr. George Campbell, Gerry D'Souza, Felicia McCurn, Iliana Limón, Dr. Ingrid St. Omer, Irma Dobbins, Jada Reese, Janis Moore, Joan Robinson-Berry, Jose Rivera, Joyce Brown, Dr. Jo Ann Charleston, Dr. & Mrs. Jonathan Earl, Dr. Joy Vann-Hamilton, Karetha Times-Marshall, Kathy April-Barr, Keith Herron, Keith Jackson, Mr. & Mrs. Kent Lovelace, Kevin Smith, Dr. Kyra Barnes Walton, LaChelle Drayton, Dr. Lawrence Norris, Leo Osgood, Dr. Lesia Crumpton-Young, Lew Shoemaker, Liz Kirby, Dr. Lynette O'Neal, Mr.& Mrs. Mai-Gemu Johnson, Marilyn Gordon, Dr. Mark Tew, Martha Artiles, Mary Waddell, Melzie Robinson, Michael Lee, Minnie McGee, Nancy Hughes, Raul Munoz, Reginald Ewing, Dr. Renetta Tull, Rick Ainsworth, Robert Ingram, Rochelle DeClue-Walker, Dr. Roosevelt Johnson, Saundra Johnson, Dr. Shannon Suber, Steven Catron, Pastor Suzette Caldwell, Teresa Bright, Terri Young, Twyla McGhee and Dr. Yvonne Freeman

I want to thank the following people who are most directly responsible for this book becoming a reality:

Cal Walker, Drs. Carl & Diann McCants, Daphne Wilson, Debra Gay, Judge Dianne Jones, Jackie Vinson, Dr. Kent Wallace, Kevin Lovelace, Kim Holmes, Larry Coleman, Madeline Powell, Maria Llopiz-Rosas Landa, Mark Dinello, Morinee Cooper, Neeka Jones, Paulette Gaines, Phae Henson, Sharon Calomese, Mr. & Mrs. Stafford Braxton, Susan Wiley, and Wanda Dennis

Last but certainly not least, I am deeply indebted to three women for making Guaranteed 4.0 and this book happen:

Thanks to Ya-Chin Chen and Dr. Tamiko Youngblood for following the system and proving that it works at all levels. Guaranteed 4.0's initial business growth is largely attributed to numerous recommendations from Dr. Youngblood. Ya-Chin's level of commitment and strategic support is immeasurable. Her vision and encouragement made this book a reality.

Most of all, thanks to Mildred E. Johnson, the best mother in the world. Words could never express my appreciation for the life you have prepared me to live. Thanks for dedicating your life to guiding and supporting your children after the death of our father James C. Johnson. Though a single mother since I was 19 months old, your strength and endurance provided the stability and security of a two-parent home. Your faith in God, positive attitude and your smile have been a constant reminder that I can do all things through Christ who strengthens me!

## Y.C. Chen

I would like to thank the following people:

- My parents who cultivated in me a strong desire to learn
- My Texas family who supported us in the long, painstaking process of writing
- All of the 4.0 administrators, students and parents who helped us to see the importance of this book
- Friends who gave their valuable time and advice
- Most of all, I am thankful of God's unconditional love and humbled by His awesome wisdom and great power to change and transform our lives.

**"Where there is no vision, the people perish."**

Proverb 29:18, King James Bible

**"If you want to have something you've never had before, you have to do something you have never done before."**

Dr. Mike Murdock
Motivational Guru & Founder of the Wisdom Center

**"Changing the world together—
one student at a time."**

Motto, Guaranteed 4.0 Learning System, LLC

# Introduction

Inventions are not always about something new. Oftentimes, innovation comes from a rearrangement of things already known. The importance of education is not news. It has been emphasized since the times of the ancient Chinese, Greeks and Romans with different learning techniques utilized. Yet, it is still necessary to explore new avenues to achieve academic success and address the needs of today's learners. There are a multitude of study skills guides and programs available today. Given these numerous alternatives, how can we guarantee a 4.0 Grade Point Average (GPA) with our method? What makes the 4.0 plan work?

The answer is truly simple: in addition to telling students "what to do," we show them "how to do it" in this proven method. The uniqueness of the program is that it is actually a system—a complete brain-based learning approach that eliminates frustration and ineffectiveness. In short, we take the mystery out of learning!

During the last 15 years, we have been sharing the Guaranteed 4.0 Learning System in 500+ live presentations. I decided to make the book available to share the 4.0 principles with more students. Throughout your reading, you may recognize many of the principles. In fact, you might even think: "This is common sense stuff!" That is completely true. While we have solid scientific research as the foundation of the program, most of the information here does not appear to be rocket science. We chose to convey the information in plain English and organized it in a format that is easy to read. Therefore whether you are a high school upperclassman, college student, cognitive scientist, psychologist, or learning theorist, you can understand and follow the 4.0 Plan.

**Here is the bottom line:**

1. **It does not matter what your academic success has been, it only matters what you want to achieve. With the 4.0 Plan, your grades are guaranteed to increase!**

2. Anyone/Everyone can follow the 4.0 Plan! If you can remember the ABC song, you can master this method.

3. You have untapped learning potential. By staying on the 4.0 Plan, you can and will become a 4.0 student!

# Our $100 Guarantee & Success Stories

* * * * * * * * * * * * * * * *

We now come to our famous $100 guarantee. Yes, you read correctly, the 4.0 Plan is guaranteed. **If you follow the 3 basic steps as outlined in this book exactly and don't earn straight A's, we will give you one hundred dollars!**

Students in 4.0 seminars always want to know: how many times we have given the $100 guarantee. The answer is zero! In the 15+ years of teaching the Guaranteed 4.0 Learning System, we have presented this seminar over 500 times. No student following the plan has ever failed to make a 4.0 GPA. This "zero-casualty" record is not because we are stingy; it is because the program really works!

Students show dramatic and sustained improvement in their GPAs. Many educators have called to say "thank-you." Parents call and cry while telling us that "Jr." is off academic probation and on the Dean's List. We constantly get e-mails, phone calls and cards from students sharing their positive experiences.

An engineering freshman, at a prestigious 4-year university, had received a 0.3 GPA at the end of his first semester in college. He had one chance to "shape up or ship out." In desperation, he attended a Guaranteed 4.0 seminar seeking help. Although he attended the seminar at midterm, he started applying the principals and still earned a 3.0 GPA at the end of his second semester. **Not only did he stay in school, when he applied the 4.0 Plan at the beginning of each semester, he achieved a 4.0 GPA every time!**

At the close of the Spring 2000 semester, Michael, a senior in accounting, learned that he was on academic probation. His grades had been adversely affected by long work hours, necessary to pay for school. He knew that he could be a more successful student but he needed to do things differently. Fortunately, Michael heard about the Guaranteed 4.0 seminar and decided to attend. To his surprise, Michael found that the seminar "was a presentation worth waking up for" on a Saturday morning. Michael improved his grades so dramatically that **he went from academic probation to the Dean's Honor List in one semester.** Needless to say, he graduated and received his hard-earned degree.

Here is Miguel Cortes' success story:

> "I had finished high school and ranked 312 out of 425. After various jobs, I decided to attend community college in 1999. Despite many hours of studying, I got a 'D' on my very first test. I was depressed and almost dropped out of school. A friend of mine taught me the Guaranteed 4.0 plan, which had helped him to get straight A's. I followed the plan and soon saw great improvements in my schoolwork. I actually spend less time studying while achieving more. On my very next test, I got an 'A'—and it was the highest grade in the class! It was that very moment that my college career and outlook changed forever.
>
> I maintained a 4.0 GPA in community college and received a full scholarship to attend Drexel University. I am now a senior at Drexel University and double majoring in Biomedical Engineering and Information Technology. My GPA is still a 4.0 and **I am poised to be the Valedictorian for the class of 2005! Furthermore, as a Fulbright Finalist, I have a full scholarship to continue my graduate studies at Oxford University, London."**

These are not isolated cases. Every year, we hear from many students who previously had doubts about finishing college and graduated with high marks. Some of them have continued on to receive Masters and PhD degrees!

Of course, we meet plenty of skeptics as well. In fact, one student was so determined to prove us wrong, he followed the plan just to show that the system could not get him straight A's. At the end of the semester we received a call of apology from this student. He sheepishly admitted that he "made a 4.0 GPA by accident!" when he followed the plan.

We have many testimonies and success stories from students, teachers and parents. To keep this book short and readable, we won't share all of them here. (You can read more stories on our website at www.Guaranteed4.com.) Please rest assured, this is a proven program with real results!

# Tips to get the most out of this book

Here are our suggestions:

- Read in a place where you can focus on the material (a quiet place)

- Instead of highlighting, jot down the important info on paper

  - Write your notes in short phrases and in your own words

  - This makes it easier to remember!

- Review the chapter outlines and practice the Guaranteed 4.0 concepts

- When you finish Part 1, keep reading to get the inside scoop from a student on how to stay on the 4.0 plan. (Basically, read the whole book.)

# Part 1

# Donna O.'s Guaranteed 4.0 Plan

**By Donna O. Johnson**

# Chapter 1

+ + + + + + + + + +

# *Stress Management*

This first chapter is about **stress management**! Why would we start this book on academic excellence with stress management? What is stress and what does stress have to do with school?

+ + + + + + + + + +

## What is stress?
## &
## What does it have to do with *school*?

+ + + + + + + + + +

It is actually quite simple—stress generally has negative affects on your grades. Based on our experience, **stress is the number one reason for poor academic performance.** It is certainly not your academic ability. Colleges and universities wouldn't admit students if they did not meet their basic requirements! Therefore, if some students are not successful, there must be other factors. We find that most students not achieving academic success simply have not found an effective way to manage stress and master the "job" of studying. Stress often keeps us from performing at optimal capacity. That is the reason we start with stress management in the Guaranteed 4.0 Learning System. After sharing how to manage stress, I will show you how to master the "job of studying."

To manage stress effectively, you first have to understand the nature of stress. **We define stress as anything that takes you away from the task at hand**. In order to make straight A's, you need about 100% of your focus on your studies. When you have stress in your life, it is very difficult to focus 100% of your attention and energy on schoolwork.

✦ ✦ ✦ ✦ ✦ ✦ ✦ ✦ ✦

## STRESS = Anything that takes you away from the task at hand.

✦ ✦ ✦ ✦ ✦ ✦ ✦ ✦ ✦

## Is Stress Normal?

In the past, I started each seminar with a stress test developed by famous psychologists and psychiatrists. The test involved questions like: "Do you ever have more to do than seemingly you have time to do?" According to the experts, if you answered "yes" to 4 or more questions out of 13, you are under significant stress!

It was almost impossible for anyone *not* to answer "yes" to at least a few of the questions on the test. In the 200+ times I gave the stress test, everyone flunked it! (The results were so predictable; I stopped giving the test.) In short, everyone is under some level of stress.

The point we are trying to make is simple: **Stress is a normal part of everyone's everyday life!** To manage stress the 4.0 way, we have to change the way we define stress. We often think of stress as major or tragic events that impact our lives, such as car accidents or a death in the family. In fact, stress can come from the "little" pressures of everyday life that cross your mind and take you off task. The truth is that everyone experiences some type of stress daily. As we often say in seminars, life is happening around us every day, and it will continue to happen.

✦ ✦ ✦ ✦ ✦ ✦ ✦ ✦ ✦

## STRESS is NORMAL!

✦ ✦ ✦ ✦ ✦ ✦ ✦ ✦ ✦

Many students have come up with creative ways to eliminate stress forever. For example, when was the last time you said to yourself in a mighty declaration: *"This weekend...I am going to get caught up!"* We often make a long to-do list and check things off as they are done. We feel pretty good about ourselves in this process. However, a week later, we become depressed when we realize more things have been added to that "to-do" list! The whole process comes to a screeching halt, until a month later when we pick up the cycle again and declare: "this weekend..."

What about this other line that we sometimes say to ourselves? *"Next semester, everything is going to be O.K.!"* Would stress really disappear and our grades magically improve when nothing else has changed? We wanted different results yet we haven't done anything differently. (I think that is the definition of INSANITY!)

Let's be honest with each other. These statements are truly counter-productive because they offer false hope. They can actually increase your stress level in the long run when the bubbles burst! So, our first task in the 4.0 Plan is to understand how to manage stress, not pretend that it will just go away one day.

## How can I manage stress?

**In this chapter, we will learn how to manage stress, instead of letting it manage us.** Many psychologists and psychiatrists have evaluated and fully endorsed our method. The Guaranteed 4.0 way to manage stress is surprisingly simple. You are going to develop a stress relieving and pre-venting activity that you can do for 1 to 2 hours every week by yourself!

✦ ✦ ✦ ✦ ✦ ✦ ✦ ✦ ✦ ✦

### Stress Relieving & Preventing Activity
**1-2 hours per week
by yourself
Both stress relieving & stress preventing**

✦ ✦ ✦ ✦ ✦ ✦ ✦ ✦ ✦ ✦

Let me explain the concept with a personal example. There are three things that really relax me: water, reading the Amplified Bible, and prayer. I absolutely love the sound of flowing water. Even when I look at a large body of water (i.e. lake or ocean), it brings an indescribable sense of peace. I also love the Amplified Bible because this translation is written in Modern English (no thee's or thou's). It also uses more words to explain the original Greek and Hebrew text. Basically, I can get more understanding and enjoy my reading. I also love to pray. Prayer helps me to realize that God is big-ger than I can ever imagine and that my problems and concerns are tiny in comparison. For me, that makes it all good. **How do I combine these three things into an activity that I can do for 1 to 2 hours a week by myself?** Believe it or not, students around the country have come up with some really creative and interesting answers to this question.

- Pray and read my Bible while getting baptized

- Swim on my back while reading my Bible & pray that my Bible does not get wet. (An engineering student actually designed a gadget for this purpose.)

- Pray while scuba diving and read a waterproof Bible.

- Skydive into the lake and pray & recite Bible verses on my way down! (I hope I will never have to do this!)

As creative as they are, these suggestions are not long-term solutions to my stress-management needs. Actually, my stress-management activity is quite simple. A couple of times a week, I take a long hot bubble bath. (I know what you may be thinking…I take showers on other days!) At least once a week, I sit in my extra-deep, extra-long Jacuzzi tub with lots of bubbles, lean on my bath pillow as I pray and read the Bible! This completely relaxes me!

But, my ultimate weekly activity is to pray in the whirlpool. I have a deal with my health club—they let me stay in the pool area 30 minutes after it closes. When everyone else leaves the water area, I get in the industrial-sized whirlpool and pray. When I get out of the whirlpool, all cares and concerns that I had just roll off me with the water droplets and go down the drain. I don't look back and literally do not stress over them anymore! For me, this is the ultimate stress relieving and preventing activity.

## TOP SECRET PHOTO

This Guaranteed 4.0 Stress Relieving/Preventing method works because it relieves stress while you are doing the activity. It also prevents stress because the mere thought of the activity can be relaxing for you. **Your stress relieving/prevention activity should be completely customized for you.** Here are some examples we have collected from various students.

- Praying while jogging

- Shooting hoops alone

- Cooking and trying out a new recipe

- Drawing or sketching

- Reading a good book

- Working out in the gym

- Playing guitar

As you can see from the examples, it is really easy to find something you can do. One important note, please do your stress management activity **by yourself.** You do not want your ability to relax to be dependent on other people. **The key here is consistent quality time by yourself!**

# Chapter I Review

We have covered three major points in Chapter I.

1.  **Stress: Anything that takes you away from the task at hand**

2.  **Stress = Normal**

3.  **Stress Relieving & Preventing Activity**
    - 1-2 hours per week
    - By yourself
    - Both stress relieving & stress preventing!

## *Guaranteed 4.0 Practice*

- Write down your stress relieving/preventing activity

# Chapter II

✦ ✦ ✦ ✦ ✦ ✦ ✦ ✦ ✦ ✦ ✦ ✦ ✦

# *Time Management*

## WHAT to do vs. HOW to do it

This is the most distinctive characteristic of the Guaranteed 4.0 Learning System. There are many study skills programs that will tell you **WHAT to do** and give you plenty of good advice. We have found that going a step further makes studying easier. We are going to show you **HOW to do it.** Instead of just telling you not to procrastinate, like you have heard a thousand times before, we will share practical step-by-step methods for time management!

✦ ✦ ✦ ✦ ✦ ✦ ✦ ✦ ✦

**You may have heard:**
Make sure you manage your time
& don't procrastinate!

**Guaranteed 4.0 says:**
Let us show you how to PLAN for success
step-by-step!

✦ ✦ ✦ ✦ ✦ ✦ ✦ ✦ ✦

## What do college students do with their time every week?

There are exactly 168 hours in every week. (It is true…you can do the math!) For many college students, it sounds like a lot of hours. Let's start with a time analysis: "What do college students do with their time every week?"

For the sake of this analysis, we will be looking at national averages for a typical full time college student who is *not* on the 4.0 plan. Don't worry if your situation is different. In Part 2, Y.C. will take you through a step-by-step procedure to create your own individual schedule.

Let's get started…

## SLEEP

Predictably, sleep is the #1 answer across the country from college students! Most people would at least like to have the opportunity to sleep eight hours a night. Well, we have good news for you; the **Guaranteed 4.0 Plan guarantees you up to 8 hours of sleep a night**. Yes, you can get eight hours of sleep a night *and* still make all A's. So, let's say we sleep 56 hours per week. I can prove that this is possible.

Here is a personal example: My freshman year in college, I went to bed at 10 P.M. every night. (Don't worry, you don't have to go to bed by 10 pm to be on the 4.0 plan—you just need to get 6 to 9 hours of sleep.) I have since discovered my natural bedtime is probably around 2:00–4:00 A.M. One of the benefits of owning your own company is the ability to set your own schedule: my office opens at noon!

When I was growing up, my mother set my bedtime at 10 o'clock on school nights. Of course, as a child, I tested the limit of my bedtime curfew by staying up past 10 o'clock to watch TV. My mother's discipline is what I would call "old-school." (My definition of "old school" is that your parents communicate both verbally and physically—smile if you can relate.) While her physical communication was never abusive, it was certainly effective! When my mother found me up past my bedtime, she would "communicate" with me! After a couple of those "physical communication sessions," my body became trained. So, even after I went away to college, my body shut down automatically at 10 o'clock to avoid pain. I am the living proof that you can sleep 8 hours per night, get all A's and still be a normal college student involved in many extra-curricular activities with a social life.

## EAT

Eating is actually the second most popular answer all over the country. Isn't that funny? Students go to college to *sleep* and *eat*! On a more serious note, people generally spend 45 minutes for lunch and another hour for dinner. We will also put in some time for breakfast since it is the most important meal of the day. This would put the estimate at about 15 hours per week.

## CLASS

The average college student takes about 15 credit hours of class per semester or its equivalent per quarter.

## STUDY

There is a national rule of thumb on studying. For each hour spent in class, you need to study 3 hours outside of class if you want to make all A's. So, here we go with 15 x 3 = 45 hours per week. (Don't get scared. We will come back to talk about this number.)

## WORK

With rising college tuition, work-study has become a significant part of the average student's financial aid package. Some students also choose to work while in school, though it is not financially necessary. We can put the average number around 10 hours per week.

## RELAX

This is absolutely critical and part of your stress management activity. After all, no one is a robot. We will estimate an hour per day for your relaxation time and an extra hour for the big weekly activity. The total comes to 8!

## SOCIAL

Here comes a popular item on the schedule. Social includes hanging out with friends, TV, email, instant messaging, phone and family. We put the estimate at 21 hours per week or 3 hours a day.

## EXTRA-CURRICULAR

Typical students spend about 3-7 hours participating in extra-curricular activities, such as professional societies, intramural sports, volunteering, etc. We will average the number at 5 hours per week. Of course, this number varies greatly from person to person.

## PERSONAL HYGIENE

Here is a non-negotiable activity! You get 1 hour a day for personal hygiene whether you think you need it or not! That is at least 7 hours per week. (Please utilize this time wisely to avoid creating any issues for your roommate or friends.)

## ERRANDS

Let's throw in 2 hours a week for errands. You may have to go to the housing or financial aid office periodically.

## EXERCISE

Let's assume you can get 3 hours of aerobic exercise each week. (Of course, the assumption behind the assumption is that you are currently exercising.)

## CHURCH / WORSHIP

This estimate varies greatly. The average number given by students in our seminars is generally about 3 hours per week.

## TRANSPORTATION

Since time to walk between classes is included in the class hour, transportation here refers to getting to/from campus and other places. We will budget 3 hours for transportation. (This number can change dramatically if you are a commuter.)

## LAUNDRY / CLEANING

We generally schedule 2 hours for both laundry and cleaning. Laundry is one of the activities that you can multi-task. (There is really no point to sit there and watch the spin cycle!)

As far as cleaning, we are about to make your parents really happy! As part of the Guaranteed 4.0 Plan, **you are going to keep your room clean everyday**! It is extremely difficult to function in an orderly fashion when there is disorder around you. A clean and orderly room will greatly help you improve your productivity!

Don't worry! This is a full-service book. We can even show you how to keep your room in order. Most of the time, there are 3 reasons your room is dirty or disorderly.

1. Piles of paper or books

2. Piles of clothes

3. Bed is not made!

In Part 2 of this book, we will show you how to make your bed in 3 seconds or less and other short cuts that are guaranteed to keep your room clean! (Please refer to FAQ #15 & 16 in Part 2 of this book.)

Now, we have finished outlining the weekly tasks and their estimated times. Let's take a look at the bigger picture.

### TIME ANALYSIS TABLE

| Activity | Time Estimate (Hours / Week) |
|---|---|
| | **Without 4.0 Plan** |
| | **168 hrs/week** |
| Sleep | 56 |
| Eat | 15 |
| Class | 15 |
| Study | 45 |
| Work | 10 |
| Relax | 8 |
| Social | 21 |
| Extra-curricular | 5 |
| Personal Hygiene | 7 |
| Errands | 2 |
| Exercise | 3 |
| Church / Worship | 3 |
| Transportation | 3 |
| Laundry / Cleaning | 2 |
| **Total Needed** | **195** |

**Wow, an average student NOT on the 4.0 plan needs 195 hours per week**. That is *27 hours* that we don't have. Remember the question on the stress test from Chapter 1: "Do you ever have more to do than you have time to do it in?"

✦ ✦ ✦ ✦ ✦ ✦ ✦ ✦ ✦ ✦

## Extra 27 Hours Needed = STRESS!

✦ ✦ ✦ ✦ ✦ ✦ ✦ ✦ ✦ ✦

**Don't get discouraged!** Guaranteed 4.0 offers a way out! We are going to review the time analysis and label all of the non-negotiable items with a star in the left column. Non-negotiable means the activitiy must be done and it must be done at a particular time.

### *SLEEP*

**Definitely a non-negotiable activity**! You don't want to get or stay on the cycle of mediocrity. The *cycle of mediocrity* is defined by the following characteristics:

- You fall asleep and miss important info in class. You have to stay up all night trying to understand what you missed in class from the book and then do the homework. Though you didn't finish the homework, you did turn it in before falling asleep in class again. Now you are so tired, you decide to skip the next class in order to get just a little nap. After all, you are too tired to pay attention anyway.

- The cycle continues. You have a chemistry test coming up. So, you drop everything and cram for chemistry. You take the exam and think you passed. Now an English paper is due. Drop everything to write the paper and turn it in at the last minute. Oh no, another homework assignment is due tomorrow that you have not started. "My group project meeting is tonight and I have not finished my part and the final project deadline is next week!" Now you wonder if you should do the homework or prep for the group meeting.

**The cycle of mediocrity starts with inadequate sleep and sucks you into a downward spiral**. You are continually tired, worn-down and stressed. It is generally a bad hair day every day, and you still only make average grades, if you pass. We call this unnecessary drama. Fortunately, on the 4.0 plan, sleep is non-negotiable and guaranteed!

## EAT

Honestly, you don't really put fork to mouth for 15 hours a week. (If you did, you would be a lot bigger, really!) Most of the time, we eat with friends or family, and mix social with eating. More often than not, we sit at the lunch table with the "coulda, shoulda and woulda" conversation. "I woulda studied but...I coulda made a better grade if...I should be studying now except I am sitting here talking to you."

✦ ✦ ✦ ✦ ✦ ✦ ✦ ✦ ✦ ✦

## *Guaranteed 4.0 Time Management Principle # 1*
## Whatever you do, do it 100%!

✦ ✦ ✦ ✦ ✦ ✦ ✦ ✦ ✦ ✦

The principle here is to fully utilize your time. When it's time to socialize, enjoy your friends 100%. Don't sit around having "coulda, shoulda, or woulda" conversations. When it is time to study, give studying 100% of your attention.

Even if you have to prepare food, we can comfortably cut this number to 8 hours per week. (We are preparing to write a Guaranteed 4.0 cookbook, with simple recipes that can produce balanced meals in 10-15 minutes or less!)

## CLASS

Non-negotiable! If you want to get a 4.0 GPA, you simply must go to class!

## STUDY

If you want a 4.0 using our brain-based learning strategies, **study time is absolutely...negotiable!** Here is the secret to the balanced life of a 4.0 student: Guaranteed 4.0 can cut your study time from 45 hours to about 25 hours. **By increasing your efficiency and effectiveness, we can reduce your study time by almost 50%.** The Guaranteed 3 steps in chapter 3 will show you how to accomplish this in detail. Please note: once you decide to follow the 4.0 plan and cut study time in half, study time becomes **NON-NEGOTIABLE!**

✦ ✦ ✦ ✦ ✦ ✦ ✦ ✦ ✦ ✦

## *Guaranteed 4.0 Time Management Principle # 2*
## ON PLAN - Reduce study time!

✦ ✦ ✦ ✦ ✦ ✦ ✦ ✦ ✦ ✦

## RELAX

That's right, non-negotiable! No one is a robot and if you refuse to relax, your body will likely take a break for you—possibly in the form of sickness.

## PERSONAL HYGIENE

Yes, non-negotiable! Stay civilized!

## CHURCH / WORSHIP

For people who go to church or practice worship traditions, this is really a non-negotiable activity. It is hard to call up your pastor or priest and ask them to reschedule service because you are going to be busy Sunday morning. It probably won't go over too well.

Let's look at the time analysis table one more time. With the changes in **EAT** and **STUDY** alone; we have reduced the schedule by 27 hours and are now even!

| | Activity | Time Estimate (Hours/Week) | Time Estimate (Hours/Week) |
|---|---|---|---|
| | | **Without 4.0 Plan** | **With 4.0 Plan** |
| | | 168 hrs/week | 168 hrs/week |
| ✸ | Sleep | 56 | 56 |
| | Eat | 15 | 8 |
| ✸ | Class | 15 | 15 |
| ✸ | Study | 45 | 25 |
| | Work | 10 | 10 |
| ✸ | Relax | 8 | 8 |
| | Social | 21 | 21 |
| | Extra-Curricular | 5 | 5 |
| ✸ | Personal Hygiene | 7 | 7 |
| | Errands | 2 | 2 |
| | Exercise | 3 | 3 |
| (✸) | Church / Worship | 3 | 3 |
| | Transportation | 3 | 3 |
| | Laundry / Cleaning | 2 | 2 |
| | **Total Needed** | **195** | **168** |

✸ = Non-Negotiable Activity

Did you notice something interesting? What is the combined total of class and study time? It is 15 +25 = 40 hours per week!

| | Activity | **Time Estimate** (Hours/Week) | **Time Estimate** (Hours/Week) |
|---|---|---|---|
| | | **Without 4.0 Plan** | **With 4.0 Plan** |
| | | 168 hrs/week | 168 hrs/week |
| ✸ | Class | 15 | 15 |
| ✸ | Study | 45 | 25 |

## 15+25 = 40 HOURS PER WEEK

Wait a minute; what does 40 hours a week sound like? It is a full time JOB! Please work with me, I want the light bulb to go on! School is really your job.

✦ ✦ ✦ ✦ ✦ ✦ ✦ ✦ ✦ ✦

### *Guaranteed 4.0 Time Management Principle # 3*

### School = My JOB!

✦ ✦ ✦ ✦ ✦ ✦ ✦ ✦ ✦ ✦

## REALITY CHECK: School is MY JOB

If we can get honest and ask ourselves one question: "Am I studying as hard as a full-time working person?" Let's also look at the flip side of the coin. When people come home from work, they generally don't take work home with them. The same principle applies to school. If we take care of school business **by following the 4.0 plan, we can have an 8:00–5:00 P.M. schedule with little or no studying on weekends!**

### *Are you working two JOBS?*

If school is your full-time job, what is the entry on the activity list called "work"? It is, in fact, a second job! Having two jobs normally presents a major challenge: people get tired, burned out, worn down and frequently have "bad hair days." The real issue is that they often don't do either job very well!

School is your full time job and I want you to do it well. Generally, people get rewarded based on how well they do their job. High school and college are not different. High GPAs are rewarded with scholarships, job opportunities, and higher salaries. In fact, the student graduating with close to a 4.0 can expect a starting salary at least $10,000 to $15,000 higher than his 2.0 counterpart. I strongly suggest making an investment in your future by staying On Plan now and reaping big time later.

Please note that "WORK" **is NOT** labeled as a non-negotiable activity. If you do not have to work, you should not work at all. How do you know if you have to work or not? Students tell me all the time that they have to work. They need money for "some pocket change" or to "make car payments." Allow me to share the 4.0 definition of "have to work." *Have to work* means you either will not have **FOOD, SHELTER, or TUITION.** If you are currently working for something other than food, shelter, or tuition, take a serious look at your lifestyle. Remember the wise saying:

> **"If you live like a (whoever you want to become)**
> **while you are a student,**
> **you will live like a student when you graduate!"**

By the way, we **don't recommend that freshmen work at all!** The transition from high school to college can be a difficult one—academically and personally. You may not want to complicate it by overtaxing yourself with work.

✦ ✦ ✦ ✦ ✦ ✦ ✦ ✦ ✦ ✦

### If you do not have to work, Do not work!

### Have to work? Only if you will not have FOOD, SHELTER or TUITION!

✦ ✦ ✦ ✦ ✦ ✦ ✦ ✦ ✦ ✦

**Have to work?** I understand the situation personally. I am the youngest of four children in my family. My father died when I was a year old. Therefore, my mother raised us with one income. By my freshmen year in college, she had already supported three children in college for three years. Money was not just tight; it was GONE! I needed to have both a scholarship and a job or I would not be in school. Given rising tuition rates, I understand the need to work. If you have to work, I encourage you to do it the right way.

If you are looking for a job while you are in school, here is the scoop.

✦ ✦ ✦ ✦ ✦ ✦ ✦ ✦ ✦ ✦

## Pick a job that will:

- **Help you now**
- **Help you later**
- **Reduce time away from studying (i.e. travel time)**

✦ ✦ ✦ ✦ ✦ ✦ ✦ ✦ ✦ ✦

"Help you now" means finding a job that can help you understand current or future classes. To "help you later" is to find a job that will look good on your resume. "Reduce time away from studying" is simple; find a job that is either close to campus or home.

For example, if you are a business major, working at a fast food restaurant as a cashier; it is not really going to help you. It does not help you with your current classes and it certainly won't do much good on your resume. However, if you worked in the college of business office, your outlook can suddenly change! You would have opportunities to develop relationships with professors and administrators. (Of course, we need to demonstrate some serious work ethic while we are working for them.) An office job in your field is much more impressive on the resume. Furthermore, it is an on campus job. This reduces travel time and shifts that time to studying as necessary.

Here is a personal example. While I did not work at all during my fresh-man year, I worked 20 hours a week every year after that. (Remember, the money was GONE!) To work the right way, I managed the tutoring pro-gram for the college of engineering. It was good management experience because I had to hire and manage 75 to100 tutors each semester. The work only required 2-3 hours per week. I simply had to be in the office the rest of the time. With my supervisor's blessing, I was able to do homework and handle extra-curricular activities during my work hours. The depart-mental secretary even typed my English papers sometimes! I got tutored at work (at no charge) and it was also one of the highest paying jobs on campus. It was not just a good job—it was the "hook up"! **Remember, if you have to work, do it the right way.**

Now we have covered all the bases. Let's move on to the rest of the Guaranteed 4.0 Plan!

# Chapter II Summary

- There are only 168 hours per week.

- Students NOT on The Guaranteed 4.0 Plan
  - Need at least 195 hours per week
  - Extra 27 hours needed = Stress

- Guaranteed 4.0 Time Management Principles
  - **Whatever you do, do it 100%!**
  - **On 4.0 Plan - Reduce study time!**
  - **School is my JOB!**
    - Class + Study = 40 hours per week!

- If you do not have to work, do not work!

  - Have to Work?
    - Only if you won't have FOOD, SHELTER or TUITION!

- Pick a job that will…
  - Help you now
  - Help you later
  - Reduce time away from studying

# Chapter III

* * * * * * * * * * * *

# *Guaranteed 3 steps to a 4.0 GPA*

## Section 1: Unwritten Rules of the Classroom

In this section, we will focus on the foundations of the Guaranteed 4.0 Learning System. Buckle up and let's get started! **Step one is highly technical**. In fact, I want 100% of your attention focused to get it down exactly…. Step 1: GO TO CLASS!

Yes, you read that correctly. GO TO CLASS. You may be wondering why I would waste time to point out such a simple fact. After all, all of us claim to understand the importance of class attendance. Yet, the formidable effect of this simple step is often underestimated. In this section, I will show you some of the secret unwritten rules of the classroom beyond simple class attendance.

Class attendance is one of the most foundational, yet most-ignored rules in college. On average, about 200 students attend a Guaranteed 4.0 seminar. When I get to this point, I often ask all of the non-freshmen students in the seminar to stand up. Then, I issue a challenge to these students: "If you've never missed a class in your college career, please remain standing." And guess what? Practically everyone sits down very quickly. I've seen seminars where **not a single student remained standing.** It does not pay to lie in this demonstration. Friends of the offenders (who know the painful truth) generally pull the lying students back down to their seats! This gives a new meaning to the term "public embarrassment"!

✦ ✦ ✦ ✦ ✦ ✦ ✦ ✦ ✦

## Step 1: GO TO CLASS

✦ ✦ ✦ ✦ ✦ ✦ ✦ ✦ ✦

This demonstration gets my point across: **many students treat class as an optional activity!** My experience is that we make bad decisions when we forget the benefits we can receive from being in class! Let's take a moment to remind ourselves of what we know so well already.

✦ ✦ ✦ ✦ ✦ ✦ ✦ ✦ ✦ ✦

## *Why should you go to class?*
## Reason #1: Because YOU paid for it!

✦ ✦ ✦ ✦ ✦ ✦ ✦ ✦ ✦ ✦

Your right to a "free" education expires once you graduate from high school (even though it isn't really free). College education is probably costing you or your family a small fortune. You should find out *just* how much one hour of instruction costs you each time you step into a classroom.

- First, calculate (or guesstimate) the amount of money you spend per semester. (This includes tuition, textbooks, room and board, pizza fund and whatnot.)

- Next, figure out the total number of hours (not credit hours) you spend in your classes per semester. The average student taking 15 credit hours spends about 210 hours in classrooms per semester. (15 hours / week x 14 weeks / semester = 210 class hours / semester)

- Finally, divide the first number by the second number. You have now calculated the cost of 1 hour of actual class time. (Are you fainting yet?)

If you did not do the tuition calculation just yet, consider these national averages:

| Type of Institution | Average Cost of 1 hour of Lecture |
|---|---|
| 2-year Community College | $ 5-10 per hour |
| 4-year Public Institution | $ 15-50 per hour |
| 4-year Private University | $ 50-125 per hour |

### Visualize this:

I am taking out a brand new $100 bill from my wallet. I am taking the bill out slowly and carefully so it stays new and crisp. To your surprise, I am placing the $100 in your hand and saying: "Keep it!" To be certain this is not a practical joke, you put the money up to the light bulb to make sure it is real. You see the strip next to Ben Franklin's face. You start to get excited because the money is real! Then I snatch the $100 from you, crumble it up, tear it in half and toss it into a nearby fireplace! You can only watch hopelessly as the $100 bill turns into a pile of ashes. Are your feelings hurt yet? You wanted to keep that $100, didn't you?

You may think: "I would never throw money away like that!" Guess again! **Every time you miss class, you are literally throwing money away!** For example, each hour of lecture costs you $50. In one week, you missed Monday's 9:00 math class because you overslept. Also, you skipped a boring lecture on Friday afternoon. (After all, who wants to spend an hour watching the economics professor drawing graphs on supply and demand?) Congratulations! You have just thrown away $100.

✦ ✦ ✦ ✦ ✦ ✦ ✦ ✦ ✦

## *Why should you go to class?*
## Reason #1: Because YOU paid for it!

✦ ✦ ✦ ✦ ✦ ✦ ✦ ✦ ✦

Let's say that you graduated from college and got a wonderful job with a great company. After receiving your big signing bonus, you pick out your dream car. It is loaded with the leather package, state-of-the-art sound system, alloy wheels and the works. You sign on the dotted line and become the proud owner of your new wheels. Now, would you leave the new car and take the bus home? Of course not! **You wouldn't because you paid for it! Be honest, you wouldn't even go to McDonald's and order a Happy Meal and NOT get your toy!**

College is the only place where people pay full price for something and they are happy when they do not get the goods. **Unlike other purchases, there are no refunds from financial aid when you miss class!** Missing class is exactly the same as purposely throwing the $100 bill into the fire. Because you are not stupid, you are not going to throw money away by missing classes. Please say out loud: "I am not stupid; I will not throw money away, I will go to class, every class, every day!"

### "Who wants to be a millionaire?"

$100 may seem like a lot of money (especially to college students), but your education is worth a lot more than $100 in the long run. How about $10,000? Consider two students that have the same major at the same university and then go to work for the same company. Student A has close to a 4.0 GPA. Student B has slightly above a 2.0 GPA. The difference in their starting salaries is at least $10,000 a year! This is only the beginning. If we calculated the salary difference over the course of an average career, the extra $10,000 grows to a mind-boggling extra $1,000,000 for student A! Please consider the extra million the next time a "friend" wants you to cut class or you want to hit the snooze button.

✦ ✦ ✦ ✦ ✦ ✦ ✦ ✦ ✦

## *Why should you go to class?*

## Reason #2: There is critical information communicated in class that you need!

✦ ✦ ✦ ✦ ✦ ✦ ✦ ✦ ✦

You should go to class because **you will receive critical information** that often makes life, *oh* so much easier. Allow me to share a real-life horror story. (Names have been changed to protect the guilty!) Jeff was in a class that met on Tuesdays and Thursdays. There was an exam scheduled for Thursday. From the syllabus, he knew that none of the material in Tuesday's lecture was going to be on that exam. Jeff was on the cycle of mediocrity and was behind in all of his classes. He decided to skip Tuesday's lecture to have more time to study. (Sound familiar?)

The test was supposed to cover chapters 3, 4, and 5. Since Jeff was short on "cramming" time, he decided to focus only on chapters 3 and 4 because chapter 5 was freshest in his memory. However, poor Jeff missed some critical information from Tuesday's class: the professor announced that he changed the exam and it would only cover chapter 5. Needless to say, when **Jeff took the exam on Thursday, his feelings got hurt!** Hurt to the point that he failed the exam and subsequently failed the class. We call this type of experience unnecessary drama! My strong recommendation is: save yourself some stress and go to class!

✦ ✦ ✦ ✦ ✦ ✦ ✦ ✦ ✦ ✦

## *Why should you go to class?*
## Reason #3: To Learn!

✦ ✦ ✦ ✦ ✦ ✦ ✦ ✦ ✦ ✦

I am overstating the obvious here! **We attend class to learn.** It can occasionally be hard to remember this between the football games and other social activities. Those buildings you see on campus have classrooms where people can in fact gain knowledge! ("Duh! I guess that's why colleges and universities are known as *institutions of higher learning!*") Believe it or not, there is actually this person in class called professor, that "theoretically" knows more than you do about the subject matter!

Students often complain: "The professor's lecture is so bad; I learn better just by reading the book." Unfortunately, that statement is simply not true. Most of us learn best when there is a combination of book reading and interaction with the lecturer and classmates. Things such as sound and sight also help us remember the material better. Learning is also enhanced when your professor explains the material differently than the book. Reading the book alone does not replace learning from classroom interaction. If that was the case, universities could simply become mail-order distance education businesses.

Additionally, most professors know when a particular student is present or not, even in large classes. If you don't believe me, take it from professors we have polled all over the country. Professors generally remember faces better than names and they identify students based on things such as their height, accent (if any), alertness, and where they sit! Attending class means giving your professor more of a chance to see you. You should show your face, ask questions, and let the professor see that you're not just another name or social security number on his or her class list.

When we say, "go to class," this includes not missing even part of a class. **Be in class 5 minutes early with paper and pen, ready to go.** If you arrive when your professor starts speaking, you are already behind in taking notes. It may take you 10 minutes to get completely caught up in the lecture. You should also pay attention to your actions towards the end of the class. Please do not pack up your belongings before the class is over (while the professor is still talking) so you can make a mad dash for the door at the end of the class! We have surveyed many professors across the country. One of their big pet peeves is: the student not paying attention and/or packing up early. This shows that the student does not value the professor's effort and time spent in class.

When you pack up early, you are distracted and run the risk of missing critical announcements. Many professors use the last 5 minutes of the class to communicate housekeeping items, such as changes to the homework assignments or information on exams. Worse yet, your actions may give the professor the wrong impression (that you are not interested in the material and simply can't wait to get out of class). If an unavoidable circumstance comes up and you have to leave early, always notify the professor before or after class and explain the situation. This is to avoid unnecessary drama; miscommunication and misunderstandings that can negatively impact your grades.

Now that we are all set to attend class, let's talk about where we should sit. **You should sit front and center!** "But...I want to sit in the back!" said one student. If someone lets you choose your own seat in your favorite music group's concert or a sporting event, would you choose the back row in the nose bleed section? No, I don't think so. You probably would fight to get as close to the front as possible and maybe a backstage pass!

✦ ✦ ✦ ✦ ✦ ✦ ✦ ✦ ✦ ✦

### *Where should I sit in class?*
### Front & Center
✦ ✦ ✦ ✦ ✦ ✦ ✦ ✦ ✦ ✦

The same principle applies here; you'll want the best seat your money can buy. In this case, **the best seats in the classroom are located front and center.** Front and center puts you in the best position to learn. These seats are known as the "Learning T." Statistically, students sitting in the front and center make A's in the class! What is so magical about these seats?

Professor

✦ ✦ ✦ ✦ ✦ ✦ ✦ ✦ ✦ ✦

## *Why should I sit front & center?*
## Fewer Distractions

✦ ✦ ✦ ✦ ✦ ✦ ✦ ✦ ✦ ✦

The first reason for you to sit front and center is: **there are fewer distractions!** Imagine being late for a movie or church service. You would probably tiptoe in the door and sit in the back to avoid drawing undue attention. You can end up being distracted throughout the event. Instead of enjoying the movie peacefully, you constantly notice all the people who are in front of you, especially if they are talking, kissing or tall enough to obstruct your view. Or, instead of focusing on the church service, you wonder about why Mr. Lee's hair looks like a toupee and why Mrs. Murphy wears that funny-looking hat! I am sure you have been distracted in this way because we all have!

Our brains are very complex and process tremendous amounts of information about our surroundings every single second. When triggered by memory, sight, sound or other conditions, our brains will generate thoughts that may not be related to the task at hand. Therefore, we are distracted. In other words, **we have enough of our own internal distractions; we don't need help from anyone else.** (Ever wonder what you are thinking about when you are not thinking about anything in particular?)

An expert said in an average classroom of students:

- 10% are interested
- 10% have no clue or interest
- 80% are engaged in daydreaming, fantasy or distracted by their surroundings

Now, keep it real for a moment. If you can get distracted while watching your favorite TV show, you can easily become very distracted during a monotone or boring lecture. (Especially if you are in a warm classroom after eating a big lunch!) By sitting front and center, you reduce external sources of distractions. This allows you to focus on the class material!

✦ ✦ ✦ ✦ ✦ ✦ ✦ ✦ ✦ ✦

## *Why should you sit front & center?*
## First Impressions

✦ ✦ ✦ ✦ ✦ ✦ ✦ ✦ ✦ ✦

Now here is one more of those unwritten rules you have been waiting for! **Make sure you sit in the front row on the first day of class.** (This should not be hard to do—the first row tends to be very empty on the first day.) Please note: When your professor walks in, he or she will scan the faces of students in the front row. Automatically, your professor assumes that these are 'A' students. Why? The professor's assumption is based on years of experience. The majority of their former A students sat front and center. To most of them, it may be a subconscious thought. But, behold the **power of first impressions!**

We know that first impressions are hard to overcome. So, ask yourself: "If my professor is going to have a first impression of me, should it be that I am an 'A' student or just an average student?" **The positive first impression has great benefits for you.** When your professor thinks that you are an 'A' student, they will treat you like one! Professors generally help students that they perceive to be 'A' students more than others. This could mean that the professor will make more eye contact with you during lecture to make sure that you understand the material. They are often more willing to offer help if you are having difficulties. They may even give some insight that comes in handy when prepping for exams.

✦ ✦ ✦ ✦ ✦ ✦ ✦ ✦ ✦ ✦

## *Why should I sit front & Center?*

### 1. Fewer Distractions
### 2. First Impressions

✦ ✦ ✦ ✦ ✦ ✦ ✦ ✦ ✦ ✦

Allow me to give you a personal example. I have been wearing glasses since I was 6 years old. I have been sitting front and center all my life just trying to see. (Thank God for thin-lense technology and cool, funky frames.) So, there I was, a freshman enrolled in an English class at the University of Texas. On the first day, my professor saw me sitting front and center and assumed I was an "A" student. The first paper I wrote, he gave me an A+!

Now the story takes an interesting turn! Have you ever read something that you did not quite understand and yet you had to write about it? That was my situation with the second paper. Call it writer's block or what have you. I was stuck for days and did not know how to write the essay. It was 11:30 the night before the paper was due and I thought I was going to die. (Remember the story from time management? I had been trained to fall out at 10 P.M.!) In my moment of desperation, I started writing down random sentences and incomplete thoughts. At this point, I didn't care anymore. I just wanted the assignment to be over. When I got to 500 words, I said, "That is all I can do!" I went to bed. When I turned the essay in the next day, I simply did not care!

However, the day I was supposed to get the paper back, I started to care again! I began to worry because that term paper was worth ¼ of my grade. During the long walk to class, I calculated worst-case scenarios: "Ok, I got an A+ on the first paper. If the professor showed some mercy, I may have a 'D' on the second one. If I get an A+ on the third paper and do extra credit assignments, maybe I can pull a 'B' out of this class!"

When I finally got my paper back, I could not believe my eyes. I really believe that it hurt the professor so much not to be able to give me an "A", he gave me a B+ instead! Underneath the grade, he wrote, "If you're having any personal problems or difficulties, please feel free to drop by my office." (This shows you how bad the mumble-jumble essay really was.)

**Why did he give me a B+ when I deserved a very different grade?** It is because he perceived me to be an "A" student! Of course, my first A+ paper proved his assumption to be true. As a result, when I failed to produce "A" work on the second paper, the professor believed that outside factors were negatively impacting my work! In short, I got the benefit of the doubt. Of course, I "handled my business" and wrote an "A" paper for my next assignment. By doing so, I confirmed the professor's first impression of me as an "A" student.

Some students ask me: "What do you do if you can't get to the class in time to get a front and center seat because of another class?" There is a simple answer to this dilemma: ask your friends to save you a seat! If this does not work, there is *one* person you can absolutely ask: the professor. Usually it's just a matter of showing him or her your schedule, describing your problem, and asking nicely. I guarantee that no one will take your seat! So, **go to class everyday, sit front and center and reap the benefits** from these unwritten rules of the classroom. Now, we move on to Step 2…

### *Step 1 Review: Go to Class!*

## Why should I go to class?

1. I paid for it!
2. Critical information is given in class that I need!
3. To learn!

## Where should I sit in class?

- Front & Center
- Sit in the Learning T!

## Why should I sit front & center?

1. Fewer Distractions
2. First Impressions

# Step 2: Secrets & Insights about Your Professor

Here we go. **Step 2: "Go See Your Professor At Least Once Per Week!"**

Every time we get to this part of the seminar, students ask: "Do I really have to see the professor?" There is an occasional moan coupled with "I don't feel comfortable talking to all my professors." Some students seem to equate seeing a professor to a trip to the dentist. **We are going to share with you special insights about your professor in this section.** I promise you that this step won't hurt a bit (or at least not as bad as your last dentist appointment).

This information will make it easier to relate to your professor and get understanding of your course material. Have you ever received second or third hand information, and then later discovered that it really didn't happen that way at all? ("Jerry said George overheard Elaine on her cell phone with Kramer and Kramer said that he told Mickey that Jerry can't remember the name of his date!")

As a result of "he-said, she-said," facts are usually distorted or critical information is missing. When you have a question about a math problem, do you want a questionable answer from your classmate or a absolute answer from your professor? The sensible choice is your professor. I want you to go straight to the source to get all your questions answered. Quite simply, your professor has firsthand information.

✦ ✦ ✦ ✦ ✦ ✦ ✦ ✦ ✦

## *Why & When Should I Go See My Professor?*

- **To get firsthand information**
- **During Professor's Office Hours (POH)**

✦ ✦ ✦ ✦ ✦ ✦ ✦ ✦ ✦

### *What is POH and why should I do it?*

Let's break it down. POH stands for Professor's Office Hours. This is a designated time that you can visit your professor. **If the office hours conflict with your class schedule, you can make an appointment.** For all practical purposes, your professor controls every aspect of the course! There is one person who knows everything you need to know in order to make an A in the class. That person is your professor. So, who should you see every week?

One of the first things that people ask: "Isn't that just brown-nosing?" My answer is "NO!" **The goal of seeing your professor is to get proper understanding of the class material.** You should go to POH to review concepts or ask questions. In addition, you will most likely develop a favorable rapport with faculty members because of your effort to learn. (That is a pretty good by-product.) Best of all, colleges and universities have made this easy. Most professors are required to set up office hours each week for students.

Many students ask me: "What if I don't have any questions?" My response is: "GO ANYWAY!" If you are not getting an "A" in that class already, it means you are missing something somewhere! If you need a starting point, gather your old homework or exams from the class. Redo the problems you missed and ask your professor if you did it right the second time!

Even if you have an A, you should still go. Another reason to go to POH is to test your understanding by explaining a concept from class to your professor. Be sure to explain the concept in your own words, so your professor can point out the subtleties you may have missed. From his or her experience, your professor can most often share helpful supplemental information. (Remember, most professors already have PhDs.)

✦ ✦ ✦ ✦ ✦ ✦ ✦ ✦ ✦ ✦

### *Need a starting point?*

- **Discuss corrected homework/exam problems**
- **Explain a concept to your professor**

✦ ✦ ✦ ✦ ✦ ✦ ✦ ✦ ✦ ✦

Generally, in undergraduate education, we learn "WHAT" to do and "HOW" to do it. In graduate school, much more focus is given to the "WHY" behind each concept. **It is always helpful to know the "why" behind the "what" in order to remember important principles.** During POH, professors have more time to explain why a particular theory or concept is valid. Once you understand the principle, you can tackle related homework or exam problems with ease. Bottom line: understanding how to apply principles is extremely beneficial for your grades.

### *3 Secrets About Your Professors*
### *(that every student should know!)*

While we are in step two, we are going to share three secrets about your professor that no one will tell you. Truly, most students never figure them out until way too late.

✦ ✦ ✦ ✦ ✦ ✦ ✦ ✦ ✦ ✦

### *3 secrets about your Professors:*
### 1. Professors are people, too!

✦ ✦ ✦ ✦ ✦ ✦ ✦ ✦ ✦ ✦

There is an urban legend that says professors are aliens who come to earth to do mind experiments on students by their long and boring lectures, impossible exam questions and 50-page research papers with a minimum of 30 references. I am happy to disprove this myth! Research on professors all over the country has shown that each of them has a human mother and father! **Yes, they are people!** Wow, this is a discovery worthy of a Nobel Prize! It stands to reason, if professors are people, it also means that **they have feelings—just like you.**

In truth, many college students do not extend the basic courtesy of considering their professor's feelings. Consider this true story as told by one professor who teaches at a prestigious 4-year university. During a German class, she heard a student say: "I hate this 'funky' German class. I wanted to take Spanish instead!" Now, let's analyze this student's situation.

Mistake #1    This professor has a PhD in German.
Mistake #2    She got her PhD in Germany.
Mistake #3    She is married to a German man!
Mistake #4    She controls the student's grade!
Mistake #5    She is the DEAN!

This true story ended with the student failing the German class (without any help from the professor). If the student had been borderline, I wonder if he would have "felt the love" from the professor's red pen!

While you may not commit grave offenses like this one, your body language may sometimes say the same thing. If you were the professor, how would you feel if a student repeatedly fell asleep in your class? Just imagine yourself as a professor for a moment. You look out into the lecture hall and all you see are: students slumping down in their chairs, some are yawning and half-asleep, and some have chin in hand just waiting for your lecture to be over. When the students do participate, they speak to you rudely as if you should pay them to sit in class. How do you feel right now as the professor? Do you still want to teach this class?

If you are the only student in your class who nods on purpose and pays complete attention to the lecture, your professor will end up teaching directly to you. Whose grade do you think the professor will be most interested in? Who can easily go to your professor for a letter of recommendation? You are right…It's all about you! When you demonstrate interest in what the professor is interested in (the course material), he or she will demonstrate interest in you (in your grade).

◆ ◆ ◆ ◆ ◆ ◆ ◆ ◆ ◆ ◆

## When you demonstrate interest, you will receive interest!

◆ ◆ ◆ ◆ ◆ ◆ ◆ ◆ ◆ ◆

We spoke to many professors and compiled a top-ten list of most offensive things students have done in class.

- Coming in 20 minutes late to class and stopping the class lecture by walking up to the professor and talking to her!
- Reading a pornographic magazine in class
- Taking off socks and propping up smelly feet
- Coming to class drunk or high
- Bringing a 6-pack to class and sharing with friends
- Hanky-panky between girlfriend and boyfriend during lecture
- Listening to loud music through headphones and asserting the freedom of expression when asked to stop
- Bringing a hyperactive dog to class
- Talking on a cell phone loudly during lecture
- Being verbally abusive toward the professor and other students

You must remember that **professors are people, too**. Most professors spend about nine years in school to earn a PhD degree. This means, they really like the subject matter they are teaching. If you display a lack of interest or disrespectful behavior in class, professors will most likely take it personally. The principle is simple—**when you demonstrate interest, you will receive interest!**

✦ ✦ ✦ ✦ ✦ ✦ ✦ ✦ ✦ ✦

### *3 secrets about your professors:*
## 2. Professor = Friend
• See professors off-line to receive more info

✦ ✦ ✦ ✦ ✦ ✦ ✦ ✦ ✦ ✦

Ok, I can almost hear the sarcastic chuckles. "Friend? Yeah, right! I don't see myself hanging out with my professor!" Allow me to define "friend" in this context. A friend is someone who cares about your well being. Here is the key: **the professor wants to help you learn!** Since you want to learn as well, this is the perfect common ground between you and the professor.

When you utilize POH, you can quickly develop a relationship. In short, your professor becomes someone who is interested in seeing you succeed in class. There are many benefits to having a professor as a friend. **When you see professors off-line, they will share more information with you than they could in class.**

Another case in point, a student shared the following experience.

> "I followed the Guaranteed 4.0 Plan and visited my professor once a week. The semester went by smoothly and I had good grades going into the final. However, something unexpected happened and I missed the final. I was really worried because the man is known for giving super hard make-up tests. I went to him to explained why I missed the final. He listened patiently and said that he knew I was a good student. He then said that **I did not have to take the exam and he would simply give me an 'A' in the class!** I was dumbfounded!"

Some people think that the student just got plain lucky. I believe that the student received favor in the situation because of her weekly meetings with her professor. The professor got to know her personally and therefore was willing to help her out of a difficult situation! **This is the power of a professor's discretion!** Have you ever wondered about the difference between a student who got 89% and received a 'B' and another student who got 87% and yet received an 'A' in the same class?

✦ ✦ ✦ ✦ ✦ ✦ ✦ ✦ ✦ ✦

## *3 secrets about your professors:*
## 3. Professor is KEY!

✦ ✦ ✦ ✦ ✦ ✦ ✦ ✦ ✦ ✦

I learned this principle from my grandmother; we called her "Mama Pearle." As you may recall from chapter 2, my mother is very "old school." Mama Pearle was old school in a different way. She never communicated physically, because she never had to. Her verbal communication was mild, concise, and infrequent. (I think she could go a whole day without saying a word!) She spoke up when her wisdom was needed. Though few, her instructions were golden and followed without question! She actually lived to be 100 years old and in my lifetime, I never heard my grand-mother repeat herself!

When I was in the third grade, I told Mama Pearle that I did not want to go back to school because I hated my teacher. My grandmother looked straight at me and said:

"Donna,
Tomorrow, you are going to school.
Tomorrow when you go to school,
your objective is not to like your teacher.
Your objective is to learn everything that she knows.
So when you master the concepts in the 3rd grade,
you will be ready for the 4th grade,
And when you master the concepts in the 4th grade,
you will be ready for the 5th grade,
and when you master the concepts in the 5th grade,
you will be ready for the 6th grade, 7th grade and 8th grade…"

Step by step, she took this speech all the way to graduate school! Then she said "and that is what you are going to do tomorrow." At the end, all I said was: "Yes, Mama Pearle." When I went to school the next day, my whole focus had changed. My objective was no longer to like my teacher or for her to like me. It was to get into my teacher's head and learn all that she knew so I could go on to the next grade. I made all As and eventually grew to appreciate my teacher.

You are not always going to like all of your professors. There are different teaching and learning styles. Sometimes, students stop going to class because they do not like a certain professor. In the end, they are the only ones being hurt by that decision. **Professors have what you need to move on to the next level!** Should you let a professor hinder your grade and ultimately your money? Your job is to get firsthand information. The professor is the key to your learning and your grade! Bottom line, the professor is the bottom line. Even if your professor is not your friend, he or she is still key!

✦ ✦ ✦ ✦ ✦ ✦ ✦ ✦ ✦ ✦

### *3 secrets about your Professors:*

### 3. Professor is KEY…
- **to my learning!**
- **to my grade!**

✦ ✦ ✦ ✦ ✦ ✦ ✦ ✦ ✦ ✦

## *Step 2 Review*

### Why and when should I go see my professor?

- To get firsthand information
- During Professor's Office Hours (POH)
  - Or by appointment

### Need a starting point?

- Discuss corrected homework/exam problems
- Explain a concept to your professor

### 3 Secrets about your Professor

1. Professors are people, too!
   - When you demonstrate interest, you will receive interest!

2. Professor = Friend
   - See professors off-line to receive more info

3. Professor is KEY!
   - Key to my learning!
   - Key to my grade!

## *Guaranteed 4.0 Practice*

- Write down professor's office hours (POH) for each class below.

## Step 3: A Proven Method for Academic Success

### Do what you are supposed to do when you are supposed to do it!

### *What are you supposed to do before going to class?*

The answer is simple: "READ!" There is an old saying: "Reading Is Fundamental (RIF)." A cliché, nonetheless it is still true. Reading the assigned materials before going to class causes you to become familiar with the terms in the book, so it will be easier to understand the professor during lecture. It is similar to seeing a movie twice. The second time you see it, it is easier to understand and remember more details. When you read the material that will be covered in class, at least 1 day prior to class, you will be able to comprehend a lot more of the related lecture. Because you now understand the class material, your homework will not take as long as before. Snap, Guaranteed 4.0 just cut your study time!

### *The real question is: Do you remember what you read???*

In 4.0 seminars, I often bet the students $100 that most of them don't know how to read. To prove my point, I ask: "How many people have ever read a chapter, closed the book, and did not remember anything that was just read?" Almost all students admit that it happens all the time! The purpose of reading is to gain understanding so you can apply it later. If you cannot retain the information, it will be very difficult to use the information in future classes, homework or exams. Guaranteed 4.0's reading method can save a great deal of time because you will actually remember the material and avoid agonizing re-reading!

✦ ✦ ✦ ✦ ✦ ✦ ✦ ✦ ✦

### *Bullet Point Reading (BPR)* Read to Remember!

✦ ✦ ✦ ✦ ✦ ✦ ✦ ✦ ✦

Our reading method is so powerful, if you just read the "4.0 way," you can earn at least a 3.0 GPA. However, this is the Guaranteed 4.0 Learning System, so we are going to stay on plan for a 4.0!

Let's say you're reading chapter 5 of a textbook that has been divided into 10 sections. Follow the BPR process.

1. **Continue reading** (in Section 1)

2. **Stop** (each time you see an important thought, concept, or definition)

3. **Summarize it in 3-5 words** (on a separate sheet of lined paper).

Now continue reading until you come to the next important part, stop reading and summarize it in 3-5 words. Keep reading until you come to the next important fact, stop reading and summarize it in 3-5 words. Repeat this process until the end of section 1. Notice that you should skip a line between each bullet point.

| **Class ABC, Chapter 5** |
| --- |
| Section 1 |
| • Hey Hey Hey Hey |
| |
| • La La La La La |
| |

**When you've finished reading section 1, you have essentially made a bullet-point outline of this section.** Now, you simply review all the bullet points created from section 1.

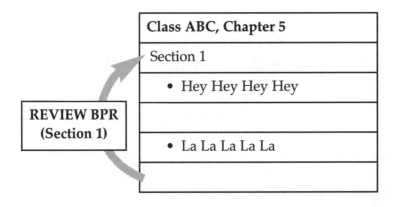

Now, we can move on to section two and repeat the same **Bullet Point Reading (BPR)** procedure:

1. **Continue reading** (in Section 2)

2. **Stop** (each time you see an important thought, concept, or definition)

3. **Summarize it in 3-5 words**

When you finish doing section 2's BPR, it is time to REVIEW! Go all the way back to the top with section 1 and **review all the bullet points in sections 1 and 2.**

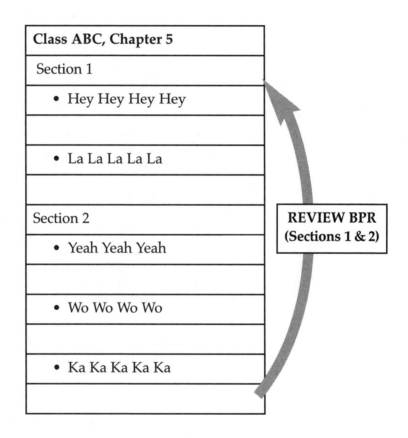

After reviewing from the top, continue to BPR in section 3. What should you do at the end of section 3? You guessed correctly! **Review all the bullet points from sections 1, 2, and 3.** The process for these first 3 sections will look like this:

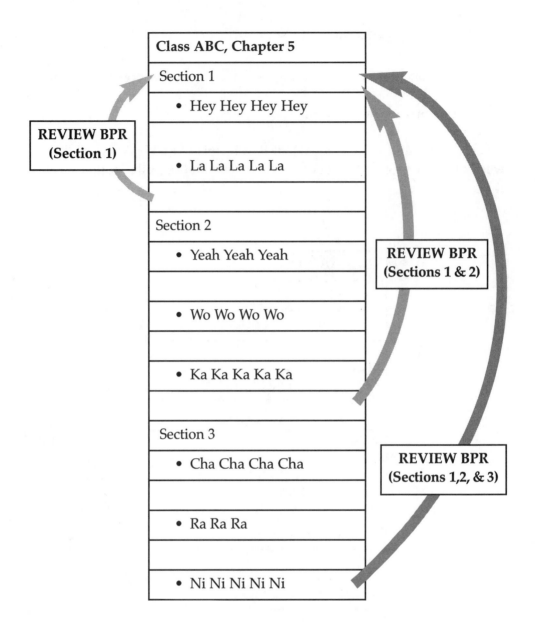

Keep repeating this process until you are finished with section 10. You will have reviewed bullet points from section 1 a total of ten times!

As you may have already noticed, BPR is done on a separate sheet of lined paper. Skip a line between each bullet point for quick, visual impact when reviewing. Please don't just scribble them in the margins of your textbook, or just go over them in your mind. When you follow the BPR process, information you read won't simply vanish into thin air!

✦ ✦ ✦ ✦ ✦ ✦ ✦ ✦ ✦

## *Definition of Bullet Point*

### 3-5 words that summarize an important thought, concept, or definition.

✦ ✦ ✦ ✦ ✦ ✦ ✦ ✦ ✦

### *Remember your ABCs?*

Remember the ABC song from your childhood? If I start singing "*A.B.C.D.,*" what is next? I am sure you are probably humming in your head: "*E.F.G.*" What if I continue with "*H.I.J.K.*"? You will reply with: "*L.M.N.O.P.*" Great job…you remember your ABCs!

Why do you remember the ABC song? I bet you did not sing it last night just for fun (unless you have younger family members who are learning their ABCs). I use the ABC song to illustrate a very important principle. You learned the alphabet because you repeated the song over and over (and over). It's all about repetition, which engraves the material into your long-term memory. Herein lies the most important Guaranteed 4.0 Principle— **Repetition over a period of time puts things into long-term memory.**

We were taught our alphabets in repeating segments. Ever notice how every-one always groups "A, B, C, D" together before moving on to "E, F, G"? It's because we were taught to repeat those letters in that same pattern: ABCD, ABCD, ABCD, —— EFG, EFG, EFG. (Is the ABC song in your head yet?)

✦ ✦ ✦ ✦ ✦ ✦ ✦ ✦ ✦

## *Guaranteed 4.0 Principle*

### Repetition → Long-term memory

✦ ✦ ✦ ✦ ✦ ✦ ✦ ✦ ✦

BPR breaks the material down into 3-5 words that are easy to remember. **The bullet points from Section 1 are equivalent to an "ABCD" segment. The bullet points from Section 2 are equivalent to an "EFG" segment, and so on.** When you do BPR and review from the beginning of section one, you are actively using the principle of repetition and putting the material into long-term memory. **BPR should be done at least 1 to 7 days before your class, giving the information enough time to sink in through repetition.** Please note: Bullet points can be done more than 1 day before going to class. BPRs can be done up to 7 days prior to class, but need to be reviewed the day before class.

✦ ✦ ✦ ✦ ✦ ✦ ✦ ✦ ✦ ✦

### *Bullet Point Reading (BPR)*

- **At least 1-7 days before class**
- **Continue reading**
- **Stop**
- **Summarize in 3-5 words**

✦ ✦ ✦ ✦ ✦ ✦ ✦ ✦ ✦ ✦

As shown by the example, **you should also skip a line between bullet points**. Visually, it is a lot easier to read BPs and review quickly when you skip a line between each BP. By reviewing BPs from different sections, your brain is learning the material as you would learn the ABC song—by repeating segments. In short, by using the BPR concept, **you'll read to remember.**

## *What are the 3 benefits of BPR?*

"Bullet-point reading" has three main benefits. **First, BPR helps you to pay attention.** Now you are reading actively with purpose. Because you have to do something as a result of what you are reading, it will be easier to maintain focus. You won't get to page 5 and realize you have just been calling words since page 2, and have to reread. Second, **BPR puts the information in your own words**. It is easier to remember your own words than someone else's. Material in your own words is familiar, comfortable, and easier to understand.

The brain remembers information best when it is in clusters of 3-5 components. When the information has more than 7 words or components, the brain has to gear up to another level and divide the information into smaller units. This is the third benefit. **BPR provides a concise "brain-friendly" information format that can easily be reviewed repetitiously.** When doing BPR, you break the info up once and for all. It will now take less brain-processing time each time you review the material.

✦ ✦ ✦ ✦ ✦ ✦ ✦ ✦ ✦ ✦

### *3 Benefits of BPR*

- **Helps you to pay attention**
- **Puts info in your own words**
- **Provides "Brain-friendly" concise format**
  - Reviewed repetitiously
  - Easily reviewed & remembered

✦ ✦ ✦ ✦ ✦ ✦ ✦ ✦ ✦ ✦

## *Here are some examples of the BPR process.*

## BPR Example # 1

### Chapter 2, Section 2-1

It is a boom time for college hoppers. Since the 1970s, the number of four-year and community college students who transfer at least once before graduation has risen from 47 percent to 60 percent of all graduates, says the U. S. Department of Education. The change is due to a 70s legislation passed by Congress to shift financial aid from institutions to individuals. As a result, this law created a generation of students with money to shop around. Just as American workers are now quicker to change jobs, students are quicker to change schools.

| |
|---|
| • **Transfer student increase** |
| • Since 70s, 47 $\longrightarrow$ 60% |
| |
| • **Reason: $ follows student** |

## BPR Example # 2

The set of real numbers contains all positive numbers, all negative numbers, and zero. Real numbers can be represented as points on a number line. You have made and used number lines in earlier mathematics courses by marking off equal distances from a starting point, labeled 0. The zero point is also called the **origin**. Numbers to the right of 0 are called **positive** numbers and numbers to the left of 0 are called **negative** numbers. Zero (0) is neither positive nor negative.

### Example 2A

| |
|---|
| • **Real # = positive + negative + 0** |
| |
| • **0 = origin** |
| |
| • **0 $\longrightarrow$ not positive, not negative** |

### Example 2B Another student chose to do this BP pictorially:

• Neg. ——————— 0 / origin ——————— Pos.

## BPR Example # 3

In 1973, Shirley Ann Jackson received a PhD degree in the area of physics from Massachusetts Institute of Technology. She is the first African-American woman to earn such an honor from MIT. In 1995, President Bill Clinton named Dr. Jackson as chair of the Nuclear Regulatory Commission, which oversees the nation-wide development of nuclear policy. She is now the president of Rensselar Polytechnic Institute (RPI), a prestigious world-renowned research institution.

| |
|---|
| • **Shirley Ann Jackson** |
| • 1973, PhD physics / MIT |
| • 1st black woman |
| • 1995, Chair, Nuclear Regulatory Commission |
| • Now, President @ RPI |

## BPR Example # 4

### Principle-Based Leadership Case Study
### Chick-Fil-A Corporation

The Sunday night gathering of Chick-fil-A employees and their family members in downtown Salt Lake City had all the makings of a church service. About 100 people, most dressed in their Sunday best, started the evening with a prayer, then listened as a Chick-fil-A employee sang a couple of Christian songs. Then, Chick-fil-A president Dan Cathy took the stage, focusing on Christianity's role in the everyday business of a fast-food restaurant chain.

"My pulpit is 20-feet wide and operates six days a week," he said, referring to countertops at each restaurant location. He detailed the company's growth in a speech peppered with scripture. He also laid out the company's mission statement: "to glorify God by being a faithful steward of all that is entrusted to us and to have a positive influence on all who come in contact with Chick-fil-A."

Cathy makes no excuses for his dedication to God. Indeed, he believes Christian principles have helped propel the growth of his business built by his father. The energetic 49-year-old Georgia native says he would rather be able to quote Jesus

Christ than Jack Welch. He carries around a small copy of the New Testament instead of the popular business book *Who Moved My Cheese*? But make no mistake. The Cathy family knows how to run a business.

Dan Cathy's father, Truett, opened the first Chick-fil-A in Atlanta. The chain steadily grew for years, expanding all over the nation—without compromising Cathy's Christian principles. The most visible component of the chain's spiritual focus is its "Closed on Sunday" policy: All of the chain's restaurants are closed on Sunday to allow employees time with their families and time to worship, if they want.

About 20 years ago, Cathy was facing external pressure to abandon his "Closed on Sunday" and other Christianity-based business practices. "Closed on Sunday" policy has cost the company deals with Disney, Six Flags, sports stadiums and malls. Cathy could have decided to give in and open his restaurants seven days a week to increase profits. Instead the company chose to stay true to its mission statement and focus on improving technology and menu selections.

According to Dan Cathy, his decision to stay true to Christian principles has paid off. Chick-fil-A is the nation's third largest fast-food chicken restaurant. The chain has 1073 restaurants in 36 states. In 2001, it reported sales of $1.2 billion. The chain on average is opening a new restaurant every week, and it recently ranked No. 1 in a trade magazine's annual report on the best drive-through in America. Of all his business accomplishments, Cathy is most proud of Chick-fil-A's scholarship programs, which have awarded more than fourteen thousand $1,000 scholarships in the last 53 years, totaling over 14 million dollars.

## Sample BPR for this case study

Refer to the chart on the next page. Please note: As the arrows indicate, the student reviewed in the middle of BPR and again at the very end. **When there are no clearly defined sections in your reading, simply review periodically as you see fit while doing BPR.**

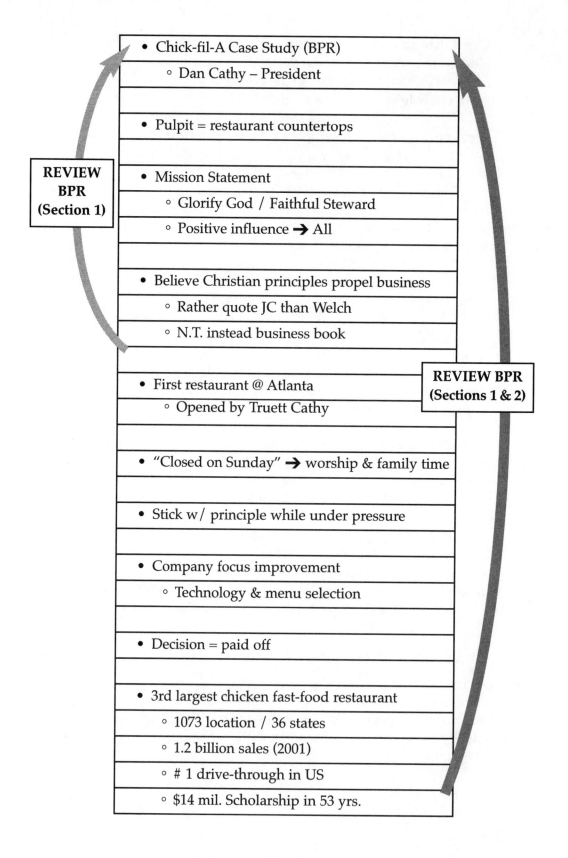

- Chick-fil-A Case Study (BPR)
  - Dan Cathy – President

- Pulpit = restaurant countertops

- Mission Statement
  - Glorify God / Faithful Steward
  - Positive influence → All

- Believe Christian principles propel business
  - Rather quote JC than Welch
  - N.T. instead business book

**REVIEW BPR (Section 1)**

- First restaurant @ Atlanta
  - Opened by Truett Cathy

**REVIEW BPR (Sections 1 & 2)**

- "Closed on Sunday" → worship & family time

- Stick w/ principle while under pressure

- Company focus improvement
  - Technology & menu selection

- Decision = paid off

- 3rd largest chicken fast-food restaurant
  - 1073 location / 36 states
  - 1.2 billion sales (2001)
  - # 1 drive-through in US
  - $14 mil. Scholarship in 53 yrs.

## *What About my Math or Science Class?*

All over the country, students always ask me: **"Will BPR work for formulas?"** The answer is: "Absolutely." Guaranteed 4.0 Learning System was originally created as an engineer's approach to learning. Almost all college disciplines use formulas of some sort. You can use the same system to deal with formulas!

Have you ever had an exam question that could easily be solved by one of the 20 formulas you learned? The only problem was that you did not know which formula to pull out of the hat. If you follow the BP format for equations, you will never again wonder what formula to use. Instead of beating your brains out to memorize formulas the night before exams, you will be able to learn how to apply the formulas.

### Bullet Point Process for Math and Science Formulas

**When doing a BP on a formula, follow these steps:**

1. **Write down the equation**

2. **BP each variable**
   - List each symbol & its meaning separately
   - Include common units in parenthesis (if applicable)

3. **Do summarizing BP(s)**
   - Ask yourself the following questions
     - To use this formula:
       — What conditions must be met?
       — What must be true?
       — What are the limitations?
   - Write down answer(s) as summarizing BP(s)

Let's look at one simple math formula: the area of a triangle. Using the BPR method, we will bullet point each symbol in the formula along with its common units.

**A= ½ x b x h**
   - **A = area ($cm^2$)**
   - **b = base (cm)**
   - **h = height (cm)**

**You want to know the common units to increase your familiarity of the formula.** This can also help you avoid potential frustration. You do not want to go through all the calculations for a math or science problem only to find that units were not properly converted prior to the calculation.

Now, take one more step in analyzing the formula. Write the summarizing bullet points. **Summarizing bullet points tell the right conditions to use the formula.** As you can see in the example, you can have more than one summarizing bullet point.

$A = \frac{1}{2} \times b \times h$

- $A$ = area ($cm^2$)
- $b$ = base (cm)
- $h$ = height (cm)
→ $b \perp h$ OR (b perpendicular to h)
→ b & h, same units

**Summarizing BPs**

These summarizing bullet points become extremely critical when you are doing homework or exams. **These bullet points give you important clues concerning when and how to use each formula.** As a result, you will remember which formula to use during exams with ease.

### Example BPR - Math / Science Formulas

$P_1 V_1 = P_2 V_2$

- $P_1$ = Initial Pressure (mmHg)
- $V_1$ = Initial Volume (ml)
- $P_2$ = Final Pressure (mmHg)
- $V_2$ = Final Volume (ml)
→ **Ideal gas @ constant temperature**

**Summarizing BPs**

$V_1 = P_2 V_2$

- $V_1$ = Initial Volume (ml)
- $P_2$ = Final Pressure (mmHg)
- $V_2$ = Final Volume (ml)
→ **Ideal gas @ constant temperature**
→ $P_1 = 1$

**Summarizing BPs**

In Part 2 of this book (FAQ #8 & 9), Y.C. will offer more tips on how to deal with multi-step math problems and using BPs to deal with long and complex multi-variable formulas. These tips will be especially helpful to students majoring in the fields of science, math, engineering and technology!

## Section Summary—I

Since we have just learned about Bullet Points, let's use them to summarize the important information in this section.

- **Bullet Point—Definition**
  - 3-5 word summary
  - Important thought, concept, definition

- **Bullet Point Reading (BPR)**
  - 1-7 days before class
  - Continual reading
  - Stop
  - Summarize, 3-5 words
  - Repeat…Finish section
  - Review from section 1

- **BPR on lined paper**
  - Skip lines between BPs

- **4.0 Principle:**
  - **Repetition → long term memory**

- **3 Benefits of BPR**
  - Helps you pay attention
  - Info → my own words
  - "Brain-friendly" concise format
    - Review repetitiously
    - Review & remember

- **BP on formulas**
  - **Write down the equation**
  - **BP each variable**
    - List each symbol, meaning & common units
  - **Do Summarizing BP(s)**
    - Questions:
      - What must be true?
      - What conditions must be met?
      - What are the limitations?
    - Answer(s) = summarizing BP(s)

## *Guaranteed 4.0 Practice*

- Practice BPR on 3 sections of a textbook chapter

- Practice BPR on 3 math or science formulas. If you are not currently taking math/science related classes, you can practice using this formula.
  - $A = \pi r^2$ (Area of a circle)

# Classroom Behavior Demystified

BPR prepares you to understand more of the professor's lecture. Now let's talk about some "unwritten" rules of the classroom that also help. Since you are paying for every class, you might as well get all your money can bring. There are three things that you need to do in class on the Guaranteed 4.0 plan.

## 1. Be Alert, Focused and Attentive

Simply put, you need to be alert, focused and attentive during class. Generally, the more physically alert you are, the more attentive you will be mentally.

**Sometimes, our body language can get us in trouble during class.** For example, some students are accustomed to slouching in their seats or using their hands to prop their heads up while they may be fully alert, focused and attentive. In reality, this type of body language is only a habit. Most people are not even aware of their actions. **However, to your instructors, this type of body language screams, " I am not interested!"**

The best way to avoid any misunderstanding is to watch what you do in class. Always sit up straight in class, and avoid laying your head on your hand. Again, these things are just habits. Habits can either be broken or reformed. The truth is, at this age, you actually don't need your hand to hold your head up—smile. If you must use your hands to prop up your head, try using fingers—it can actually give you a more interested and intellectual look than before.

## 2. Be an Active Participant

Another way to learn more in class is to be an active participant. Asking and answering questions and volunteering represent active participation. In addition to showing professors that you are interested, you can increase your attention span and information retention by actively involving yourself in class.

Many times, students don't want to ask questions because they are afraid of looking stupid. If this is your fear, simply remember this tip. **If you have a question during lecture, about 1/3 of the class has the same or a similar question regarding the subject matter.** By raising your hand and asking the question, you will receive the correct answer firsthand from the professor. You will also help other students in the classroom!

### 3. Take Accurate Notes

Accurate notes are not an exact record of the professor's words. Have you ever attempted to write down everything a professor said word for word? Most students end up with pages of incomplete sentences and no real understanding of the concepts taught. This is generally a desperate, mindless activity with hopes of one day understanding. The Guaranteed 4.0 procedure to take accurate notes is: **listen first, understand the concept, and then write it down**.

Most professors conduct their lectures by introducing one principle at a time. They then explain the principle further with examples or various demonstrations. **This "principle/example" cycle can run a couple of times during a typical class.** This is where your BPR comes in handy; since you are already familiar with the terms and information, it becomes easier to concentrate on the lecture. When the professor gives different examples to support the principle, you will not mistake them as separate ideas and become confused. BPR makes the note-taking process easier and more meaningful.

✦ ✦ ✦ ✦ ✦ ✦ ✦ ✦ ✦ ✦

## Three Things in Class

- Be Alert, Focused & Attentive
- Be an Active Participant
- Take Accurate Notes
  - Listen first
  - Understand
  - Write it down

✦ ✦ ✦ ✦ ✦ ✦ ✦ ✦ ✦ ✦

### *What should I do with my class notes?*

In this section, we are going to cover the secret to organizing class notes—Bullet Point Notes (BPN). So far, you have learned about Bullet Point Reading (BPR at least 1-7 days before class), and the three things you should do in class. Now, immediately after class, I want you to do a bullet point outline of your class notes. **The process is called Bullet Point Notes (BPN).**

✦ ✦ ✦ ✦ ✦ ✦ ✦ ✦ ✦ ✦

## Bullet Point Notes (BPN)

- Immediately after class
- Continue reading (class notes)
- Stop
- Summarize, 3-5 words

✦ ✦ ✦ ✦ ✦ ✦ ✦ ✦ ✦ ✦

Immediately after the class is dismissed, take your class notes and begin doing BPN. **You will follow the same process as BPR.** While reading over page 1 of your class notes, summarize each important thought, concept and definition in 3-5 words. When you are finished with BPN for page 1 of your notes, go back and review all the bullet points created from page 1. **Remember to BPN on a separate sheet of paper.**

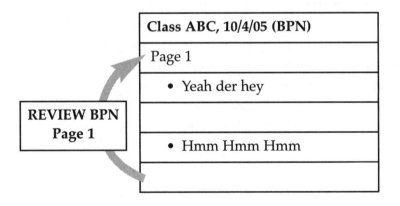

| Class ABC, 10/4/05 (BPN) |
| Page 1 |
| • Yeah der hey |
| |
| • Hmm Hmm Hmm |
| |

**REVIEW BPN Page 1**

Now, do your bullet point notes for page 2. When you are finished with page 2 BPN, go back and review all BPN from pages 1 and 2.

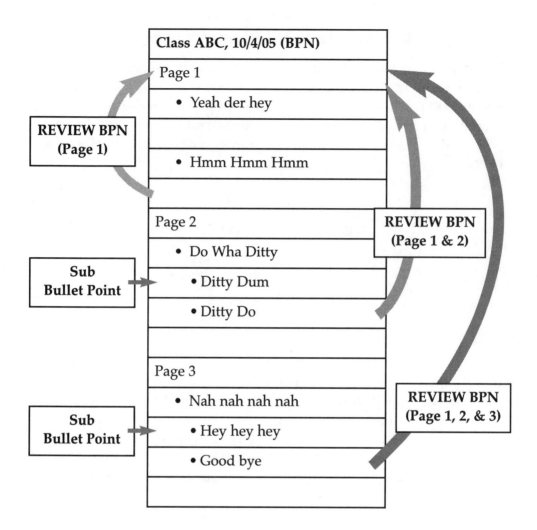

You may notice that BPN for pages 2 & 3 look different than for page 1. These are **Sub Bullet Points.** Whenever you have information that takes more than 5 words to summarize, simply use a heading and put the related information as sub bullet points below it. You may have multiple sub bullet points. Please note that you should **not** skip lines between sub bullet points. This is done to keep and organize related material together in the brain.

**We are *not* asking you to simply rewrite all of your notes**. That would take too much time. While most of your lecture notes contain important information, a professor may teach a major principle and then use several examples to clarify. In this case, simply do a BPN on the major principle and possibly one or two examples to refresh your memory. **BPN usually takes about 5-15 minutes for an hour of class.**

### Reasons for doing BPN immediately after class

Why is it important to start bullet-pointing your notes immediately after class? **It helps to capture the material while it's still fresh in your memory.** The probability of retaining information greatly increases the sooner you repeat it. For example, it is common after meeting someone to forget their name. But, if you immediately repeated their name when you met them or wrote it down, you'd be much more likely to remember. The 4.0 system allows you to see the same material several times in different ways. If you have a schedule conflict and cannot BPN immediately after class, please do so as soon as possible that day.

By doing BPN, you can reinforce the various concepts you learned in class. Who knows? You may even discover that you do not understand something as much as you thought. By realizing this early on and utilizing your professor's office hours (POH), you will have a much easier time completing your homework later. You will not end up in a situation where you are trying to teach yourself the material again.

## *The Sequence of the 4.0 Plan*

If you haven't noticed yet, we are **systematically** going through a particular sequence of events. To summarize in a timeline, the process looks like this so far.

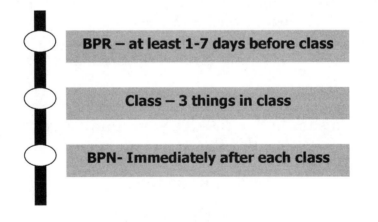

**BPR – at least 1-7 days before class**

**Class – 3 things in class**

**BPN- Immediately after each class**

## *Help! I procrastinate!*

✦ ✦ ✦ ✦ ✦ ✦ ✦ ✦ ✦

*Guaranteed 4.0 says:*

**Simply start your homework the day it is assigned!**

✦ ✦ ✦ ✦ ✦ ✦ ✦ ✦ ✦

In the Guaranteed 4.0 system, **you will start your homework the DAY it is assigned.** Please note that start does not mean you have to finish the first day. Most college assignments are not due the next day. We've all heard horror stories of students staying up all night to complete a week's worth of math problems the night before they are due. We all know the drill. After trying to do the homework problems for a couple of hours, we conclude that there is no hope. We then spend hours on the phone, playing 'Six Degrees of Separation' to find the student who would let us see their homework! (If I am reading your mail, don't freak out. Just keep on reading and pretend you have never done this before…)

Sometimes, students tell us that they stay up all night doing homework. That does not make any sense at all! They waste 50% of the night trying to stay awake by drinking coffee, jolt cola or whatever. They then spend another 25% of the time strolling through the dorm looking for the unfortunate soul who will listen to them complain about how much work they have to do. They may even do some work in the last 25% of the night. The sad truth is that at midnight by your body clock, you lose at least 50% of your brain's efficiency and productivity. You will spend 20 minutes doing something that would only take 10 minutes when you are fully rested. In short, "all-nighters" are not worth it!

This kind of unnecessary drama can be easily avoided by **starting** homework the day it is assigned. Remember that I am only asking you to **start the homework** the day it is assigned; not finish the homework. This way, you can pace yourself and actually observe the "20-minute rule."

✦ ✦ ✦ ✦ ✦ ✦ ✦ ✦ ✦ ✦

## When should you START your homework?
The day it is assigned!

### The 20-minute Rule

- Stuck on a homework problem
- More than 20 minutes
- Skip the problem
- Go to POH & get help

✦ ✦ ✦ ✦ ✦ ✦ ✦ ✦ ✦ ✦

## The 20-Minute Rule

When doing homework, you want to observe the 20-minute rule. Assuming you have done all the things described earlier and **you are still stuck on a homework problem for more than 15-20 minutes, skip the problem and go see the professor.** If you give a solid 20-minute effort, and still have no clue on how to proceed, you are probably missing a rule of thumb or something fundamental. So, instead of hurting yourself, you should cut your losses and skip that problem. Sometimes 5 minutes with your professor can answer all your questions about the homework. Remember, the purpose of POH is to get firsthand information from the professor!

Now, you can see how starting the homework the day it is assigned and the 20-minute rule work hand in hand. When you start your homework early, you have time to practice the 20-minute rule and get help. If you start an assignment at midnight the night before it is due (sound familiar?), you definitely can't call or email your professor if you run into unforeseen difficulties. (If you call your professor and wake up his or her spouse, it may be a guaranteed 'F' for you!)

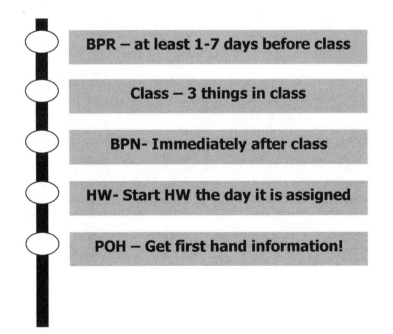

BPR – at least 1-7 days before class

Class – 3 things in class

BPN- Immediately after class

HW- Start HW the day it is assigned

POH – Get first hand information!

## *Section Summary—II*

- **3 things while in class**
  1) Alert, Focused & Attentive
  2) Active Participant
  3) Accurate Notes: Listen, Understand, Write

- **Bullet Point Notes (BPN)**
  - Immediately after class
  - Continue reading
  - Stop
  - Summarize, 3-5 words
  - Repeat...Finish page
  - Review from page 1

- **Homework (HW)**
  - Start, day assigned
  - Avoid unnecessary drama

- **The 20-minute Rule**
  - Stuck on a homework problem
  - More than 20 minutes
  - Skip the problem
  - Go to POH & get help

# Understanding the principles with Bullet Point Concepts (BPC)

## The Secret to analyzing homework & exams

Because you are on the 4.0 plan, you actually will finish your homework before it is due. You're ON PLAN! Now, what should you do with returned HW? The same thing you've been doing with everything else, bullet points. The last BP, **Bullet Point Concepts (BPC)**, is the difference between an 'A' and a 'B' for most students.

## Importance of BPC

In high school, getting good grades on tests sometimes depends on the students' ability to memorize the material. It is a completely different ball game in college. On college exams, your professors don't expect you to simply repeat the class and textbook examples, or to regurgitate the homework. College professors prepare exams to test the student's ability to apply principles and concepts. They expect you to understand the why behind the concepts learned and then apply those principles to solve future problems. Doing BPC will make sure you know how to apply your knowledge. That is why we can guarantee you a 4.0 when you are ON PLAN!

## How do you BPC?

When you get corrected homework or exams back, **review EACH problem and answer the question: "Why is this the correct answer?"**

You want to understand *why* it's the correct answer and then summarize it in BP format. If a problem is not correct, first find the right answer then do your BPC. If you don't know the correct answer, you can POH and ask for the answer key to your homework or exams before you BPC. **Also, make sure you BPC all problems, not just the ones that were marked wrong.** By doing BPC, you will know the "WHY" behind every single homework problem and question. Once you have completed and reviewed your BPC, acing similar problems on future homework or tests will be easy!

✦ ✦ ✦ ✦ ✦ ✦ ✦ ✦ ✦

### Bullet Point Concepts (BPC)

- On corrected HW & Exams
- Answers the Question: "WHY?"
- "Why is this the correct answer?"

✦ ✦ ✦ ✦ ✦ ✦ ✦ ✦ ✦

## BPC Example #1- Math

Let's practice with a really simple math question,

$$1 + 2 \times 3 = ?$$

At first glance, someone may answer 9 by mistake. Actually, 7 is the correct answer. Now to do the BPC on this problem, we have to ask: **"Why is 7 the correct answer? "**

We may answer the question several ways and each answer can be a BPC.

- **Order of operations**
- **Multiply 1st, Add 2nd**
- **P.E.M.D.A.S.**

Note: P.E.M.D.A.S., also known as "Please Excuse My Dear Aunt Sally," stands for parenthesis, exponents, multiply, divide, add, and subtract.

There are virtually unlimited numbers of combinations for simple math problems like this. You wouldn't memorize the exact math problem for an upcoming test! (Can you imagine how crazy you would feel if you tried to cram $1 + 2 \times 3 = 7$ into your head?) **With BPC, you examine the *why* behind the right answer**. Now you can solve any similar math problems with ease.

## BPC Example #2- English

Let's look at an English example together. Please choose the correct verb.

**People is/are always speaking incorrectly.**

The answer is "are" for this sentence.

Your BPC may look like one of these:

- **Subject-Verb Agreement**
- **People = Plural → ARE**

## BPC Example #3- Chemistry

Why don't we do a more collegiate example? Let's say you are taking chemistry and your homework includes writing the molecular structure of soap. (I use soap for this example because hopefully it is something we are all familiar with.)

Soap works because it has two ends. One end of a soap molecule is hydrophilic. (Hydrophilic means that it likes water.) The other end is hydrophobic; you guessed it; it does not like water! The end that likes water (hydrophilic), attaches to the water coming out of your showerhead. The end that does not like water (hydrophobic), likes dirt and grease. Guess what? It attaches to your skin! The end that likes water is stronger and pulls the other end off your body, along with dirt and grease. Then it all goes down the drain with the rest of the water. Now you can say: "Aha! I know how soap facilitates the cleansing process!"

After you have correctly answered a homework problem about the molecular structure of soap, you are ready to do BPC. You want to know *why* soap works. You can rewrite the molecular structure again just for repetition, but the critical thing is to understand and remember that soap works because it has 2 ends. So, the BPC for soap can simply look like the diagram below:

**SOAP BPC:**

### True Story about the SOAP BPC

There was a bonus question on a chemistry exam. Of course, it was a really difficult bonus question. The professor wanted to see if his students could think outside of the box and apply principles. Therefore, he purposely wrote a graduate level word question that undergraduate students would not understand. His only clue was a line at the end of the long paragraph: "It has a soap-like structure." This triggered a Guaranteed 4.0 student's memory and she wrote down the soap BPC on the exam paper. (She was hoping for some partial points!) Much to the student's surprise, the professor awarded her the full bonus points for picking up on the clue and solving the problem to his satisfaction! This example demonstrates why BPC is often the difference between an A+ and a B.

Students often ask me in seminars: "What happens if my professor doesn't return exams?" My classic answer always has been: "Who is your friend? And, who do you see every week?" There are many reasons that your professors may not return exams. However, remember that professor = friend. All you have to do is ask. If your professor is still uneasy about returning the exam to you, there is still another option. You can always ask your professor to allow you to review the questions and do BPC during office hours. The benefits of understanding the principles on old exams in order to apply them to future problems far outweigh any temporary inconveniences. By the way, your professor will most likely be impressed by your persistence and desire to learn as well! This is a win-win situation!

## *A secret weapon to stay on top of it all*
### - Bullet Point Notebook

You have 3 types of Bullet Points: Bullet Point Reading (BPR), Bullet Point Notes (BPN) and Bullet Point Concepts (BPC). **Keep all of your bullet points in a Bullet Point notebook and take it with you everywhere!** This gives you the flexibility to review BPs at any convenient time. You will still keep other notebooks for your class notes and assignments. **Please note: The only thing in your bullet point notebook should be bullet points.**

✦ ✦ ✦ ✦ ✦ ✦ ✦ ✦ ✦

### Bullet Point Notebook

- Organize all BPs ➜ In 1 Notebook
  - Take it everywhere
  - Review repetitiously

✦ ✦ ✦ ✦ ✦ ✦ ✦ ✦ ✦

You can't carry all of your textbooks with you all the time. But, you can definitely take a BP notebook with you everywhere you go. Your BP notebook gives you a snapshot of all your classes. By having an organized BP notebook, you have all the important info from all classes. Remember, your BPR is an outline of important textbook material. BPN are done on your class notes and BPC covers your returned homework and exams. You are set!

**Take all opportunities to review your BPs.** For example, if your friends were 10 minutes late to meet you, instead of getting upset or twiddling your thumbs, just review BPs! Not only are you not wasting time, but you are also preparing yourself for an A+ finish.

## How do I organize my BP notebook?

To correctly organize your BP notebook, you need the following material:

- One 3-ring binder (1" or 1½")

- 3 dividers with tabs per class (So, if you have 5 classes, 15 individual dividers are required.)

- 1 self-adhesive tab per class (So, if you have 5 classes…you probably already did the math, 5 tabs are needed.)

For each of your classes, you should have 3 dividers labeled: BPR, BPN, BPC on their vertical tabs. You also need 1 horizontally self-adhesive tab to identify the subject matter. The subject tab should be attached to the first divider for that class, which is BPR.

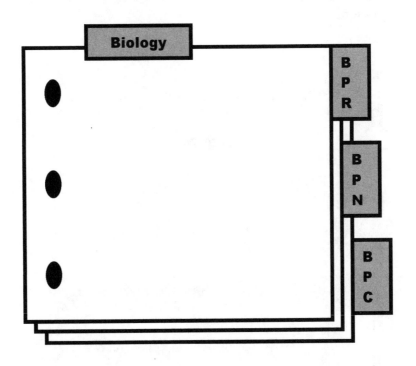

After repeating the process, you will have a set of dividers labeled BPR, BPN, and BPC for each class. Then put these dividers into the 3-ring binder. Voila, you now have a BP notebook. **You can now put all BPs into their appropriate spots and review them repetitiously!** (For your convenience, we have custom dividers with BPR, BPN, BPC already printed on them. Check out www.guaranteed4.com for more details.)

**The BP notebook is your secret weapon to staying ready for quizzes and exams.** Come on, let's face it, all of us have crammed for an exam and done well. But, there is a major drawback to cramming. The information is only in short-term memory, soon to be forgotten after the exam. It may be easier in high school than in college. However, you can end up paying a high price when midterms and finals come. You can stay up studying 3 days and nights and still feel utterly unprepared for comprehensive exams. There is too much information to cram into your head in such a short period of time. **Using the Guaranteed 4.0 Plan, you will never have to cram for an exam again.** Repetition over a period of time puts things into long-term memory! By reviewing repetitiously, you will actually learn the material and be able to remember it. You will be amazed by how easy it will be to prepare for final exams. Studying is a pay me now or pay me later scenario. If you pay now (study now by following the 4.0 plan), you pay less. If you pay later (study later by cramming), you will ultimately pay much more. I suggest that you pay now and save yourself some time, stress, and money!

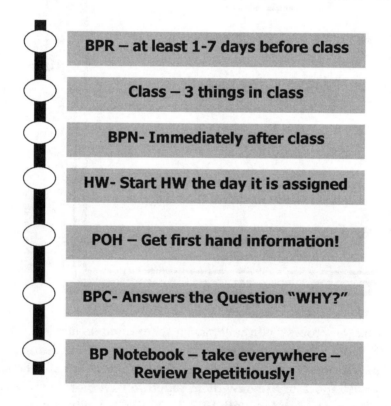

BPR – at least 1-7 days before class

Class – 3 things in class

BPN- Immediately after class

HW- Start HW the day it is assigned

POH – Get first hand information!

BPC- Answers the Question "WHY?"

BP Notebook – take everywhere – Review Repetitiously!

## *Section Summary -III*

- **Bullet Point Concepts (BPC)**
  - On corrected HW & Exams
  - Answers the Question: WHY
    - WHY is this the correct answer?

- **BPC**
  - Understand principles for future application
  - Why vs. What
  - Secret to analyzing Exams / HW
  - Difference between A+ and B

- **BP Notebook**
  - 1 BP Notebook → all BPs (BPR, BPN, BPC)
  - Only bullet points in BP notebook
  - Take it everywhere
  - Review repetitiously

# 3 things about the word "study"

## *That every college student should know*

✦ ✦ ✦ ✦ ✦ ✦ ✦ ✦ ✦ ✦

### *First thing about study:*

## Study at a consistent time & consistent place

✦ ✦ ✦ ✦ ✦ ✦ ✦ ✦ ✦ ✦

I actually learned this principle from my former assistant pastor. She presented a series entitled: "Lord, Teach us to Pray!" There was one thing she taught in that series that I never forgot. She said to have a consistent time and consistent place to pray. As a result of the message, I designated a chair in my room as my "prayer chair."

Every time I see that chair, I think about prayer! Every time I sit in that chair, I am praying! Every time I pass by that chair and I have not been in that chair for a while…well, it makes me think that I should be praying. The chair literally represents PRAYER to me! When I sit in that chair, I don't have to get all geared up to pray. I don't get distracted by food or telephone calls. When I sit in that chair, my body is already PRE-CONDITIONED to PRAY because that is the only thing I do in that chair!

The same principle applies to studying. **When you establish a consistent time and consistent place to study, you are pre-conditioning your body to study more effectively.** You actually create a habit of studying. A habit is something that you can do that does not require as much conscience thought as other actions. For example, you have a habit of eating. When your favorite meal is placed in front of you, no one has to remind you to pick up your silverware and bring food to your mouth. It is a habit that you do without much conscious thought. Studying also becomes a habit during that specific time and at that particular place.

Be honest with yourself, if you sit down to study for 2 to 3 hours, how long does it usually take you to get into gear? The average answer all over the country is: **30-45 minutes** before being completely engaged in productive studying. But, when you have a consistent time and consistent place to study and are pre-conditioned to study, the results are quite different. **It now only takes 5-10 minutes to engage in productive studying!** Studying at a consistent time in a consistent place will drastically cut your studying time.

Some students have said: "I don't know if I have the discipline to do that." Guess what? Once you start following the plan, your brain will take over and help you! Before you know it, you will have established the routine! For example, remember that plate of your favorite food set before you. You don't have to gear up and teach yourself how to eat again? NO! Your pre-conditioned response is to open your mouth, chew, and swallow and lick your fingers if necessary! It is just that simple. **We are going to harness more brainpower to work for us!**

❖ ❖ ❖ ❖ ❖ ❖ ❖ ❖ ❖

## *Second thing about study:*
## Study in a conducive place"

❖ ❖ ❖ ❖ ❖ ❖ ❖ ❖ ❖

You should study in a place that is conducive to studying. **A conducive place means that it lends itself easily to the act of studying.** There are many places that can be conducive for one student but totally disastrous for another. Some students study well in the library. My friend Gary could sit in the library and study for three hours without moving or being distracted. (I can't sit anywhere for more than 15 minutes without distracting myself.) But, a lot of students sit in the wrong spot in the library—by the newspaper/magazine/internet-enabled PC tables where everyone lingers. Before long, students with good intentions of studying find themselves caught up in conversation, email or the latest web video. Those spots are not conducive for them.

If you stop for a moment and are honest with yourself, you can probably figure out the places that are really conducive for you to study. My freshman dorm room was conducive place for me to study, but only during the day. It was not conducive at all during evening hours. I lived on the first floor of a dorm that housed 3,000 people. All my friends knew that I had food in my room and had to pass by to and from the elevator. In the evening it became Grand Central. But, during the day everyone was in class or out and about on campus. So, I studied between classes in my room and finished all my homework before the evening hours.

As you can see by now, what is conducive depends on your individual circumstances. So, instead of a discussion on "conducive places to study," I actually want to focus on the places that are not conducive!

Most of us lie to ourselves: *"I just have my TV on for the background noise while I am studying!"* The truth is that if you have the TV on, you generally only remember *during commercial breaks* that you were supposedly studying. This is especially true of your favorite show. Do yourself a favor by being honest, just schedule TV time and watch your favorite show! Let's not pretend to study during that time just to ease a guilty conscience.

*"What about listening to music while reading?"* Here is what generally happens to me (and many other students): my foot starts to tapping, my head and body start to "groove" with the rhythm, before I know it, I grab my imaginary microphone and pollute the air-quality with my off-key singing! As we said before, stress is anything that takes you away from the task at hand! **Listening to music can take your focus away from studying** and create stress (for you and possibly your roommate). So keep it real; does your music distract you?

The biggest myth (or lie) I want to address in this section is: *"I can read this chapter sitting up in my bed!"* Please, we all know the drill on this one! You start in an upright position in your bed. Minutes later, your bed puts your brain into "sleep mode" and you scoot down to a more comfortable spot. Your bed is the consistent place you sleep at a consistent time. So, your brain and body are sending the following messages back and forth:

"We are in bed now…
We sleep here…consistently…
We are getting sleepy…really sleepy…
You need a nap… Sleep induce now…"

Eventually, you have the book flat on the bed while propping your head up with your hand. That is what we called a PDP: "pre-drooling position." You are about to drool all over the textbook that you paid too much money for!

**STAY OUT OF BED WHEN STUDYING!** It will work wonders for your productivity!

✦ ✦ ✦ ✦ ✦ ✦ ✦ ✦ ✦

## *Third thing about study:*
## No compromise!

✦ ✦ ✦ ✦ ✦ ✦ ✦ ✦ ✦

**No compromise means that you are on the 4.0 plan and you study with other people who are on plan!** Here is a simple quiz: if you want to make A's, who should you study with? People who make A's! Who should you study with if you want to make B's? People who make B's! (We won't go any lower!) **There is no compromise! People who study together generally make the same grades.** If you want your 4.0, don't do anything that hinders the new 4.0 way of learning.

If you don't know anyone who is on the 4.0 plan at your school, you can either "be an army of one," encourage your friends to read this book or you can teach them the plan. (However, if you give them the $100 guarantee, it is on you!)

**Sometimes, tough decisions may have to be made regarding your study group**. Let's say that you, John, and Christina formed a 4.0 study group. Three weeks later, John got discouraged. He said: "I don't want to do the 4.0 plan anymore…too many BPs." At this juncture, you and Christina should encourage John as good friends would. Starting anything new can be difficult. It is perfectly normal and you should do your best to support John. However, if two weeks later, John kept on complaining and was not making the effort to be on plan; it is time to kick him to the curb!

The principle is this: "If someone who you study with decides to deviate from the plan, let him or her go during study time." **You need to focus on purpose.** If John refused to honor the purpose of the study group— getting a 4.0, he doesn't fit into your and Christina's academic plan. All three of you can still hang out, go to the movies and have fun. Nevertheless, you and Christina should make it absolutely clear that John can't be a part of the study group, unless he is willing to be get back on the 4.0 plan!

Remember, one thing always leads to another. Those students who compromise on "little things" (such as POH) will soon find out that they have compromised the bigger picture of their academic success!

## *Section Summary—IV*

- **3 things about the word "study"**
  - Consistent time & place
  - Conducive place
  - No compromise

1. **Consistent Time & Place**
   - Prayer chair
   - Pre-conditioning saves time
   - 5-10 minutes to productive studying

2. **Conducive Place**
   - Individual situation
   - No TV, music
   - No studying in bed

3. **No Compromise**
   - Stay on Plan
   - Study with others on plan
   - Focus on purpose: 4.0 GPA

## *Guaranteed 4.0 Practice*

- Identify a consistent time and place that is conducive to study

- Identify 2-4 people that could be part of your 4.0 study group

# Chapter IV

✦ ✦ ✦ ✦ ✦ ✦ ✦ ✦ ✦ ✦ ✦

# *Final Declaration*

Make a promise to yourself and I want you to say this out loud! **I will never, ever, and ever STUDY AGAIN!**

The word "study" is simply too vague. Before the Guaranteed 4.0 plan, students would tell me that they studied all day long. But, it only meant they had a book open somewhere all day. They may have been on the phone talking about how much work they have to do, watching TV, or taking a nap. From now on, I want you to strike the word "STUDY" from your vocabulary.

## NO MORE "STUDY"!

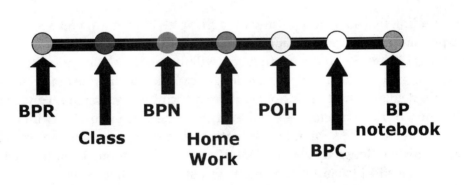

## "ON PLAN!"

We are going to use our new concrete language: BPR, Class, BPN, HW, POH, BPC and BP Notebook. These seven terms will replace the word study. Our "on-plan-ness" is easy to measure using this system. Just ask yourself the following questions:

1. Did I BPR at least 1-7 days before class or not?
2. Did I go to class and arrive 5 minutes early or not?
3. Did I BPN immediately after each class or not?
4. Did I start the HW the day it was assigned or not?
5. Did I visit POH this week for every class or not?
6. Did I BPC my returned HW and exams or not?
7. Did I take my BP notebook everywhere or not?

Here you have it—7 easy questions. It's simple, to stay on plan and get a guaranteed 4.0!

I have what I call the "5 questions of life" and I always share them at the end of every seminar.

✦ ✦ ✦ ✦ ✦ ✦ ✦ ✦ ✦ ✦

## Donna O.'s 5 Questions of Life

- What do you want?
- What are the challenges you will face?
- How can you meet those challenges?
- What do you have to give up to get what you want?
- Is it worth it?

✦ ✦ ✦ ✦ ✦ ✦ ✦ ✦ ✦ ✦

By reading this book and putting the principles to practice, you are expressing the desire for academic excellence—a 4.0 GPA! While pursuing this goal, there are no doubts that you will face many challenges—both external and internal. External challenges can include friends not on plan, family demands, and professors that are difficult to understand. However, the most difficult challenges are the internal ones. "Can I do it? Will I be able to get a 4.0?" I submit to you that **you can meet and overcome every academic challenge by staying ON PLAN!** As I mentioned before, it will take some effort to start something new. I strongly believe everyone can do the plan. I am asking you to follow the Guaranteed 4.0 plan for at least 21 days to break any old/ bad study habits and form the new positive habit of being ON PLAN!

So, what do you have to give up to get what you want? (We don't generally like this question.) It is not sleep. It is not even a social life. The answer is simple: give up the old concept of STUDYING! Are you going to give up the old mindset of "studying"? Are you willing to get off of the cycle of mediocrity and get into a proven system of success? If you are willing, get ON PLAN! Is it worth it? I guarantee that you will be pleased with your decision to stay ON PLAN!

One of my favorite inspiring sayings is a biblical scripture: "Therefore, if any person is in Christ, he is a new creation; the old has passed away, the new has come" (2 Corinthians 5:7). I use this scripture as an analogy for the Guaranteed 4.0 students at the end of every seminar.

**If you follow the Guaranteed 4.0 plan,
You are a new student and
that old student with average grades
no longer exists.**

**You are now a new student
on plan making easy A's .**

**It does not matter where you are coming from academically,
it only matters where you want to go!
BE ON PLAN!**

***Guaranteed 4.0!!!***

# Part 2

# Applying the 4.0 Plan— A Student's Perspective

By Y.C. Chen

# Introduction to Part 2

✦ ✦ ✦ ✦ ✦ ✦ ✦ ✦ ✦ ✦ ✦ ✦ ✦ ✦ ✦

Welcome to Part 2 of the Guaranteed 4.0 Plan. This part is specifically written to answer frequently asked questions and to address common situations students face. My goal is to make it easy for you to use the 4.0 principles effectively.

**What qualified me to write Part 2 of this book?** I have firsthand experience in following the Guaranteed 4.0 Plan. I attended a Guaranteed 4.0 seminar the weekend before my freshman year in college. However, as a prideful freshman on scholarship and majoring in architecture at an elite institution, I thought I knew it all and did not need any help. To be honest, the purpose of my attendance was not academic. I simply wanted the $100 and the free home-cooked lunch that was promised on the flyer. (If you have experienced college dorm food, you can understand my ulterior motives.) As a result, much of the information in the seminar was promptly forgotten as soon as I woke up from my free-lunch-induced nap.

The tables soon turned by the third week of school. **I was a living example of the "cycle of mediocrity"** that Donna O. so accurately described. Sleeping only 4 to 5 hours a night, I was studying harder than ever before yet dangerously close to losing my scholarship. (I needed to keep a 3.0 GPA!) Out of desperation, I contacted Donna O. for some advice and she was gracious enough to help me implement the Guaranteed 4.0 Plan. **Believe it or not, I actually made a 4.0 GPA that semester by following the plan!** Not too bad considering that almost half of my classmates dropped out of school or changed majors! I would have been included in that statistic if I had not followed the Guaranteed 4.0 Plan!

Throughout college and graduate school, I always got straight A's in the semesters that I was ON PLAN. However, I would periodically get a big head by taking short cuts and not following the plan entirely. Bad idea! Those bad decisions did not get me A's, so I quickly amended my ways! (Trust me, you do not want to be praying for God's mercy as you read your report card at the end of semester.) Thanks to the 4.0 plan, I did well in school overall: my undergraduate GPA was 3.8. I also received a 3.9 GPA for my MBA degree!

These Frequently Asked Questions (FAQ) are compiled from my real-life experiences and actual questions students have asked Guaranteed 4.0 staff members. As I answer these FAQ, you will see how easy it is to stay on the Guaranteed 4.0 plan. I sincerely hope these answers will help you stay ON PLAN!

Y.C. Chen

# Frequently Asked Questions (FAQ)

**FAQ #1** The plan worked because you are smart. Will it work for me?

**FAQ #2** The professor gives us his lecture notes or power point slides. Do I still have to take notes and BPN?

**FAQ #3** When should I BPN if I have classes back to back?

**FAQ #4** It takes me longer to read with BPR; what should I do?

**FAQ #5** How does the principle of "starting the HW the day it is assigned" apply to a long-term project?

**FAQ #6** How can BPs help me write an essay?

**FAQ #7** Help! My professor does not speak English!

**FAQ #8** Can you show more examples of BPs for math problems?

**FAQ #9** How do you BP really long and complex formulas?

**FAQ #10** When should I study for an exam?

**FAQ #11** How do I deal with test anxiety?

**FAQ #12** What are some test-taking strategies BEFORE the exam?

**FAQ #13** What are some test-taking strategies DURING the exam?

**FAQ #14** What are some test-taking strategies AFTER the exam?

**FAQ #15** How do I make my bed in 3 seconds or less?

**FAQ #16** How can I keep my room clean?

**FAQ #17** How do I manage my time on the Guaranteed 4.0 plan?

**FAQ #18** How do I catch up without falling behind?

**FAQ #19** I just learned the 4.0 plan and I have a test this week; what can I do?

**FAQ #20** If I have questions after reading this book, who can help me?

## *Frequently Asked Questions*

### FAQ #1   The plan worked because you are smart. Will it work for me?

Many students take one look at my Chinese face and assume that I am smart! (Or they assume, I am good at math and I can do all that stuff seen in a bad Kung-Fu movie.) Let me help you out—forget all those stereotypes! I did not learn English until 7th grade. So, I actually had challenges beyond course content. If the Guaranteed 4.0 plan worked for me, it will definitely work for you!

**The 4.0 plan works because it taught me how to learn!** Guaranteed 4.0 uses brain-based learning strategies. The Bullet Point system helps you put information in a format that your brain can process quicker. It is also easier for you to remember. That means you can use more of your brain's power to learn more effectively.

If you still think my story is unique, allow me to share one more success story. Tony enrolled in a 4-year institution conditionally as a "special student." University administrators wanted to see his first semester's academic performance before admitting him to a regular degree program. Tony attended a Guaranteed 4.0 seminar and was motivated. He said that he really got his inspiration from the session and was admonished to do well by following the plan. He took 12 credit hours of classes that semester and received a 4.0 GPA!

### FAQ #2   The professor gives us his lecture notes or power point slides. Do I still have to take notes and BPN?

Many professors make their power point presentations available on the Internet prior to class or distribute a lecture outline during class. When students rely solely on the given outline, they often become passive listeners and miss critical information from the lecture! It may be convenient to refer to the professor's outline but **it is not a replacement of your class notes nor your BPN.**

During lectures, professors often cover more information than included on the outline and show various examples. Professors can also have certain gestures or body language that emphasize the importance of a topic. Taking notes during lecture allows you to benefit from these important additional details! (If you wish, you can take notes directly on the printed presentation or lecture outlines.) In addition, BPN offers a quick and concise way to capture all the knowledge you learned during class. It will check your understanding and make doing the HW much easier.

## FAQ #3  When should I BPN if I have classes back to back?

If you have two classes back to back, do the BPN *after* the second class for both classes. Please do not BPN during your next class. (Unfortunately, some students have tried this.)

If you have 3 or more classes back to back, the first thing you want to do is change your schedule, if it is possible. Many students love the idea of scheduling as many back-to-back classes as possible because it opens up the rest of the week. However, the side effect can be a significant reduction in your productivity and ability to learn. It is a simple fact, that when you have been bombarded by huge quantities of different information in a short period of time, you simply do not learn as well. Without mental breaks, you are just not as ready and fresh to learn in that 3rd or 4th class, as you would be in the first.

If a schedule change is not possible, my suggestion is to take a 5 to 10 minute mental break after your last class before doing BPN. You should take that short break in the classroom, not wandering around campus or going to the cafeteria where you will get distracted. After your break, you will be better equipped mentally to do BPN for all previous classes! Remember, BPN only takes 5-15 minutes per hour of class.

## FAQ #4  It takes me longer to read with BPR; what should I do?

Anytime we learn to use a new tool, it always seems to take longer than before to perform a similar task. In actuality, BPR may take longer in the beginning. With minimal practice, the BPR process can be easily mastered and it will actually save you time in the long run.

1. BPR helps to focus your attention so you read effectively. It actually can increase your reading speed.

2. You won't have to waste time re-reading the material.

3. Reviewing BPR also helps to put the information in long-term memory. Therefore, it can save you time and energy when you are doing homework or prepping for exams.

**One mistake students often make is writing down too much information in their BPR.** Remember, only do BPR on important (or testable) information. You can always show your BPR to your professor and ask if you are summarizing the relevant information. I had a history professor who reviewed my BPs and told me what he considered to be important. **Remember, BPs are not complete sentences.** (This is slightly counter-intuitive to years of English classes.) Keeping BPs less than 5 words allows your brain to process and store the information much better and faster.

In short, BPR is the foundation of the Guaranteed 4.0 Learning System. If you BPR properly, you can expect at least a B average! But, follow all 3 steps and get your 4.0.

### FAQ #5 How does the principle of "starting the HW the day it is assigned" apply to a long-term project?

The average college student panics when he or she realizes that there are only two weeks left before the research paper, which was assigned at the beginning of the semester, is due. The procrastinating mentality of "I can do it later" has been exercised. Seriously, when was the last time that "later" ever came?

The same principle of starting your homework the day it is assigned applies here as well. For example, if you have to do a research paper, you can still start this long-term paper the day it is assigned. You can do one of the following things:

1. **BP the instructions and suggestions from the professor**
2. **Start a list of potential topics**
3. **Identify possible resources**
4. **BP any initial ideas/thoughts**
5. **Put together a plan with a timeline**

It is very important to BP and follow your professor's instructions. You don't want to lose points on technicalities. (For example, some professors require students to follow a specific writing format, such as MLA or APA.) The day the term paper is assigned, students often have ideas that are forgotten by the time they actually sit down to write the paper. Keeping a list of potential topics will solve that problem. By the way, never start writing a term paper unless you have checked your topic with the professor. I once finished 75% of a term paper without checking with the professor. Imagine the horror when I found out that my professor did not like the research topic. I frantically rewrote the entire term paper in 7 days. That was unnecessary drama!

## FAQ #6    How can BPs help me write an essay?

The Guaranteed 4.0 essay strategy is simple and can save you considerable time. Essays are normally written about something you were required to read. Many times, the instructor will share the essay topic with students prior to assigning the required reading. **Your first step is to do focused bullet points (BPs) on the book or article that you are reading.** By keeping the paper topics or goals of the reading in the back of your mind, you only have to BP the relevant information that you would consider including in your paper. You don't need an outline of the entire book with every detail or fact. You are basically focusing your reading to look for and do BPs only on things that may help in the essay-writing process.

After the reading is complete, **the next step is to brainstorm with BPs**. This is where BPs will help your creative juices to flow with ease. While you brainstorm, you can use BPs to document various ideas from different sections of the reading materials, class notes, discussions with your professor or classmates, etc. You can do this either with paper or directly in a word-processing program. (Personally, I prefer paper because I enjoy the freedom to doodle and draw as I think.) Don't worry about grammar or references at this point, just focus on putting down your ideas in BP format. Remember, a BP has 3-5 words.

**The third step is to structure the essay with BPs.** When you review your BPs from the brainstorming sessions, you will easily discover some BPs have related ideas. Begin by clustering BPs with similar ideas or themes. Then write a sentence from each bullet point. Or, simply take each BP and write a sentence with it in your own words, before clustering. **Either way works!** The process is flexible and you can decide what is best for you.

**The last step is to formulate different paragraphs and the essay.** After turning your BPs into sentences, you simply arrange them into paragraphs that make sense. Don't worry if the paragraphs seem disjointed right now. As you reorder the paragraphs into an essay, you will begin to write the necessary transitions to make it a cohesive paper with an introduction and conclusion.

**The essay-writing process is now made simple because you have a step by step plan that helps you start to finish.** In addition, you have documented and clarified your ideas with BPs, sentences and paragraphs. You will never waste time just staring at a blank computer screen again!

✦ ✦ ✦ ✦ ✦ ✦ ✦ ✦ ✦ ✦

## *Writing Essay with BPs*

1. **Do focused BPR on reading material**
2. **Brainstorm with BPs**
3. **Structure eessay: BPs into sentences**
4. **Formulate paragraphs → paper**

✦ ✦ ✦ ✦ ✦ ✦ ✦ ✦ ✦ ✦

**Please allow the simplified example below to illustrate the procedure.**

### Assigned Reading:

*Fish is Fish* (Lionni, 1970) describes a fish that is keenly interested in learning about what happens on the land, but the fish cannot explore land because it can only breathe in water. It befriends a tadpole that grows into a frog and eventually goes out onto the land. The frog returns to the pond a few weeks later and reports on what he has seen. The frog describes all kinds of things like birds, cows and people. The book shows pictures of the fish's representations of each of these descriptions: each is a fish-like form that is slightly adapted to accommodate the frog's descriptions. For example, people are imagined to be fish who walk on their tailfins, birds are fish with wings, cows are fish with udders. The tale illustrates both the creative opportunities and dangers inherent in the fact that people construct new knowledge based on their current knowledge.

*Fish Is Fish* is relevant not only for young children, but for learners of all ages. For example, college students often have developed beliefs about physical and biological phenomena that fit their experiences but do not fit scientific accounts of these phenomena. These misconceptions must be addressed in order for them to change their beliefs.

### Essay Topic

In the Guaranteed 4.0 book, the authors urge the readers to let go of the old concept of "studying." Based on the information given above, explain in 2-3 paragraphs the importance of giving up the old mindset of "Studying" while being "On Plan."

## 1) Do focused BPR on Reading Material

| |
|---|
| •Fish is fish (Lionni) |
| • Fish befriends tadpole ➜ frog |
| • Returns from land, describes experience |
| |
| • Fish's interpretation of frog's description |
| • Everything ➜ all fish like |
| • People = Fish walking on tailfins |
| • Birds = Fish w/wings |
| • Cows = Fish w/udders |
| |
| • Principle ➜ opportunities & dangers |
| • Constructing new knowledge on current understanding |
| |
| • Relevancies: learners, all ages |
| • Example: College students |
| • Hold beliefs - physical & biological phenomena |
| • Fit personal experiences, not scientific facts |
| • Addressing misconceptions: change student's beliefs |
| |

## 2) Brainstorm with BPs

Students organize their ideas in different ways. On the next page is an example of my brainstorming session. I wrote down several ideas as they came to mind in BP format. Then, I grouped similar ideas using arrows and circled the idea chosen for the thesis statement (please see next page).

## 3) Structure Essay: BPs into Sentences

## 4) Formulate paragraphs ➜ paper

The writing process is as individualized as it is creative. Therefore, we won't actually write the whole essay for this exercise. If you understand the principles and examples shown in Step 1 and 2, you are well on your way to a great essay!

- Relating <u>Fish</u> to 4.0 = How?

- From book: Give up "study"

- Study—Too general / fuzzy

- 3 things about STUDY
  1. Consistent time / place
  2. Conducive
  3. No compromise

- 5 questions of life
  - see book for questions

- Give up <u>old mind set</u>— "studying"
  - Give up old ways of thinking
  - Become new students

- 4.0 / On-Plan things
  - bpr, class, bpn, hw, poh
  - BPC & BP notebook
  - DOJ: "concrete & measurable"

- **4.0 → Address misconceptions of "study"**
  Change my belief on study

- Article: fish-like people (?)

- Theme: Building new on old knowledge

  - Creative yet dangerous
  - Why? Misinterpretations

- Old mind set
  → study / old knowledge

- 4.0 plan: new knowledge
  - link? New knowledge fish gained.
  - ANSWER TO ESSAY / THESIS!

- Getting new knowledge (4.0 plan)
  - Different from old plan
  - or Non-existing study plan!

Danger: based new knowledge / 4.0
  - on old knowledge / study

- **Why?**
  - **Misinterpretations?**
  - **Not following the plan?**
  - **Not learn as much ?**
  - **Learn the wrong thing !!!**
    - **Is that possible?**

- MY LINK: old vs new
  - Build new on old
  - Ex: 4.0 on old mindset

- Problem: learn the wrong thing
  - or not learn as much
  - not as effective in learning

## FAQ #7   Help! My professor does not speak English!

Some students have said in seminars: "My professor doesn't speak English! How can I do POH?" In this case, it's even more important to remember that professors are people, too! Imagine you are a world-renowned researcher who is invited to teach in a foreign country where the language is not your native tongue. You are nervous and fully aware that to them you have a heavy accent. Your audience is frustrated about your lack of ability to communicate and they are not hiding their feelings at all. Pretty horrible scenario, huh? Yet, it accurately reflects most foreign professors' experiences.

Think of it this way, the professor who does not speak English well actually speaks multiple languages. English may not be his or her second or third language. (Changed your perspective a little, didn't it?) Donna O.'s mom always says, "kill them with kindness." That's right, a little kindness goes a long way. So, when you POH you should not come with the attitude of: "What is wrong with you? Why are you teaching in America and you can't even speak English?" Remember, **they are people with feelings—just like you and me**.

It is essential that you speak to your foreign professor outside of the classroom. **In his or her office, the professor will tend to be more relaxed.** For many professors, one-on-one interaction tends to be more comfortable than lecturing in front of a large audience. (If you have any experience with public speaking, you know what I am talking about!) You will find that the professor's accent is not as thick and his speech slows down as well. Once you understand your professor, you will find that there is a wealth of knowledge that he or she can share with you.

## FAQ #8   Can you show more examples of BPs for math problems?

Here is an example from a math textbook:

The slope of a line is a number that describes its steepness. It is the ratio of the changes in y (rise) to the change in x (run). The slope, m, of the line joining any two points $(x_1, y_1)$ and $(x_2, y_2)$ in the xy-plane is given by:

$$m = \frac{(y_2 - y_1)}{(x_2 - x_1)}$$

Using the equation, the slope of the line joining (-3,-1) and (1, 5) is

$$m = \frac{(y_2 - y_1)}{(x_2 - x_1)} = \frac{(5 - (-1))}{(1 - (-3))} = \frac{6}{4} = \frac{3}{2}$$

### Example Bullet Points (Student A)

$$m = \frac{(y_2 - y_1)}{(x_2 - x_1)}$$

- $m$ = slope / line steepness
- $x_1$ = x-coordinate, point 1
- $y_1$ = y-coordinate, point 1
- $x_2$ = x-coordinate, point 2
- $y_2$ = y-coordinate, point 2
- → Line must join two points  ←——————— | Summarizing BP |

### Example Bullet Points (Student B) – familiar with XY coordinates

$$m = \frac{(y_2 - y_1)}{(x_2 - x_1)}$$

- $m$ = slope
- $(y_2 - y_1)$ = change in rise: y-coordinates
- $(x_2 - x_1)$ = change in run: x-coordinates
- → 2 points, XY plane  ←——————— | Summarizing BPs |
  - → Straight line

## FAQ #9   How do you BP really long and complex formulas?

In the previous question, we used a simple slope formula to illustrate our answer. Please make sure you review and understand these principles before reading any further.

Many college students will eventually face long and complex formulas that have more alphabets and symbols in them than numbers. This is especially true if you are majoring in math, science, engineering, technology-related fields or doing graduate work. While the same BP principles apply, the approach is slightly different.

✦ ✦ ✦ ✦ ✦ ✦ ✦ ✦ ✦ ✦

## BP process for complex formulas

**1. BP each variable**
**2. BP each cluster**
**3. Summarizing BP – story, meaning & limitations**

✦ ✦ ✦ ✦ ✦ ✦ ✦ ✦ ✦ ✦

Let us take a hypothetical formula for example:

**Formula # 1**    $Y^*_1 = (\mu_1 k + \gamma_1) / (\beta_1^{T_1})$

### 1) BP Each Variable

$Y^*_1 = (\mu_1 k + \gamma_1) / (\beta_1^{T_1})$
- $Y^*_1$ = Yield ratio (adjusted), sample 1
- $\mu$ = Utilization index
  - $\mu = \phi - \lambda$
  - $\mu \neq 0$
- k = dreser's constant (- 0.5362)
- $\gamma$ = Yield ratio (unadjusted)
- $\beta$ = Beta Strength Indicator
  - $\beta$ can be negative
- T = Time lapsed, specific to sample

> **BP Each Variable**

In this step, you choose the degree of detail you need to see for each variable. In addition to doing BPs for each variable, this student used sub-BPs to define certain vairables in greater detail:

a. For the utilization index, sub-bullet points were used to indicate how $\mu$ is calculated ($\mu = \phi - \lambda$) and its limit ($\mu \neq 0$).

b. k is identified as the "dreser's constant" with a negative numerical value. (Doesn't it come in handy on the exam to have that number in long-term memory?)

### 2) BP each cluster

A cluster is defined as a group of information within the formula. There can be many clusters in a complex formula. Again, you can decide what constitutes a cluster as you BP. It all depends on your familiarity with the material. Continuing with our example:

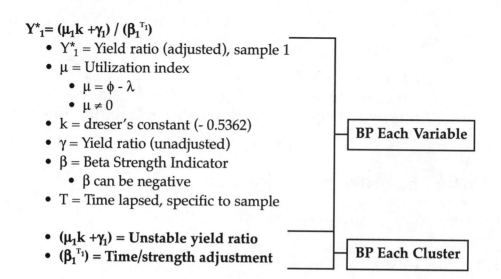

$Y^*_1 = (\mu_1 k + \gamma_1) / (\beta_1^{T_1})$
- $Y^*_1$ = Yield ratio (adjusted), sample 1
- $\mu$ = Utilization index
  - $\mu = \phi - \lambda$
  - $\mu \neq 0$
- k = dreser's constant (- 0.5362)
- $\gamma$ = Yield ratio (unadjusted)
- $\beta$ = Beta Strength Indicator
  - $\beta$ can be negative
- T = Time lapsed, specific to sample

- **$(\mu_1 k + \gamma_1)$ = Unstable yield ratio**
- **$(\beta_1^{T_1})$ = Time/strength adjustment**

BP Each Variable

BP Each Cluster

### 3) Summarizing BP– story, meaning & limitations

Each formula serves a purpose, tells a story, or gives a description of the process. Instead of forcing yourself to memorize the alphabets and numbers in the formula, simply focus on understanding the "big picture." You will then be able to apply the formula in future scenarios. It is also important to know the limitations of the formula. Let's go back to our example:

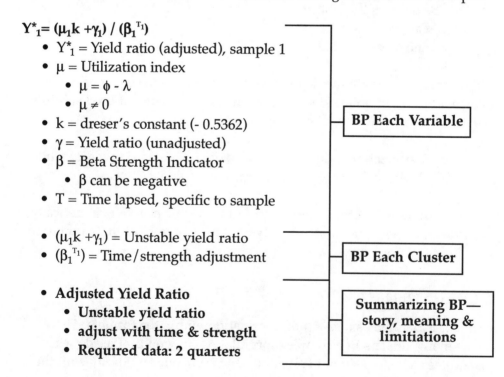

$Y^*_1 = (\mu_1 k + \gamma_1) / (\beta_1^{T_1})$
- $Y^*_1$ = Yield ratio (adjusted), sample 1
- $\mu$ = Utilization index
  - $\mu = \phi - \lambda$
  - $\mu \neq 0$
- k = dreser's constant (- 0.5362)
- $\gamma$ = Yield ratio (unadjusted)
- $\beta$ = Beta Strength Indicator
  - $\beta$ can be negative
- T = Time lapsed, specific to sample

- $(\mu_1 k + \gamma_1)$ = Unstable yield ratio
- $(\beta_1^{T_1})$ = Time/strength adjustment

- **Adjusted Yield Ratio**
  - **Unstable yield ratio**
  - **adjust with time & strength**
  - **Required data: 2 quarters**

BP Each Variable

BP Each Cluster

Summarizing BP— story, meaning & limitiations

At first glance, it may seem like a horribly long process. However, you now have an accurate understanding of each variable, cluster and the application of the formula. **Doesn't it help to remember the formula as well as knowing how to use it on a future homework or exam problem?**

A set of BPs for a complex formula would look something like this:

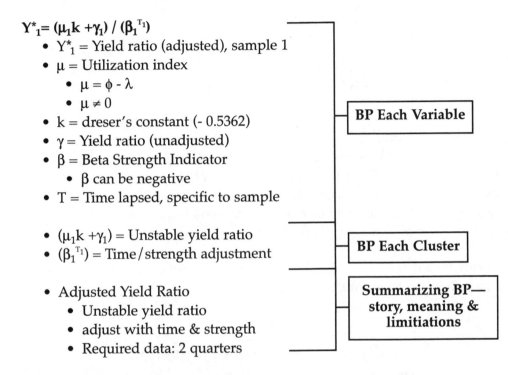

$$Y^*_1 = (\mu_1 k + \gamma_1) / (\beta_1^{T_1})$$

- $Y^*_1$ = Yield ratio (adjusted), sample 1
- $\mu$ = Utilization index
  - $\mu = \phi - \lambda$
  - $\mu \neq 0$
- k = dreser's constant (- 0.5362)
- $\gamma$ = Yield ratio (unadjusted)
- $\beta$ = Beta Strength Indicator
  - $\beta$ can be negative
- T = Time lapsed, specific to sample

**BP Each Variable**

- $(\mu_1 k + \gamma_1)$ = Unstable yield ratio
- $(\beta_1^{T_1})$ = Time / strength adjustment

**BP Each Cluster**

- Adjusted Yield Ratio
  - Unstable yield ratio
  - adjust with time & strength
  - Required data: 2 quarters

**Summarizing BP—story, meaning & limitiations**

Here is another benefit of doing BPs on long and complex formulas. Many formulas build on each other. This is generally a good thing except when you do not understand the fundamental concepts of the formulas. **Our method will help you to easily master one formula after another.** Consider another complex formula for example:

**Formula # 2**   $$Y^*_{1+2} = ((\mu_1 k + \gamma_1) / (\beta_1^{T_1})) + ((\mu_2 k + \gamma_2) / (\beta_2^{T_2}))$$

Doesn't this formula look familiar? It is basically an extension of the previous one. However, if you had not done BPs on the previous formula, formula #2 would probably look like a whole new formula. This can create some serious stress in your life. Here is an example of how BPs can really help to reduce unnecessary stress.

$$Y^*_{1+2} = ((\mu_1 k + \gamma_1) / (\beta_1^{T_1})) + ((\mu_2 k + \gamma_2) / (\beta_2^{T_2}))$$

- $Y^*_{1+2}$ = Adjusted Yield Ratio (2 samples)

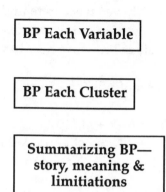

- $((\mu_1 k + \gamma_1) / (\beta_1^{T_1})) = Y^*_1$
  - Adj. yield ratio (sample 1)
- $((\mu_2 k + \gamma_2) / (\beta_2^{T_2})) = Y^*_2$
  - Adj. yield ratio (sample 2)

- $Y^*_{1+2} = Y^*_1 + Y^*_2$
- Required data: 2 quarters (both samples)

Since BPs were done for variables such as $\mu$, k, $\gamma$ and $\beta$ in the previous formula, this student chose not to rewrite them. (However, you can always rewrite them to reinforce your long-term memory.) The student also recognized the "big picture" pattern within the formula that $Y^*_{1+2} = Y^*_1 + Y^*_2$. In other words, it is as easy as 1+1 = 2. Once you learn to recognize and analyze these patterns, right answers are just around the corner!

**In conclusion, when you are dealing with long and complex formulas, BPs will prove to be your best friends!**

✦ ✦ ✦ ✦ ✦ ✦ ✦ ✦ ✦

## *BP process for complex formulas*

1. **BP each variable**
2. **BP each cluster**
3. **Summarizing BP – story, meaning & limitations**

✦ ✦ ✦ ✦ ✦ ✦ ✦ ✦ ✦

### FAQ #10  When should I study for an exam?

Now for the big question—when should I study for my exams? **The answer is NEVER!** With Guaranteed 4.0, you are systematically preparing for exams as you BPR, BPN, BPC, go to class, do HW and utilize POH. The information you learned is being committed to your long-term memory through the review process. Before an exam there is no reason to cram or panic because you have actually already learned the material!

All that is left for you to do is review BPR, BPN and BPC in your BP notebook. You should also work extra problems for speed and accuracy. In a history class for example, it may be sufficient just to review bullet points from class. For the calculus exam, you may want to work different problem types, in addition to reviewing bullet points. So seriously, no more all night study sessions! They are now a thing of the past!

## FAQ #11 How do I deal with test anxiety?

Test anxiety is a common issue among students. Students often report extreme nervousness, emotional roller coasters or the dreaded "blank-out" effect before and during exams. Test anxiety causes stress because it takes you away from giving 100% of yourself while prepping for and taking exams. Many times, students have adequately prepared for an exam, but that little nagging / worrying voice in the back of their minds actually sabotages their effort by causing test anxiety. On the Guaranteed 4.0 Plan, **test anxiety can be greatly reduced or even eliminated by doing 3 things:**

### 1) Enjoy your weekly stress relieving /preventing activity.

These activities are helpful because they prevent stress from building up to the point where it becomes anxiety. If possible, schedule a special session of your stress relieving / preventing activity the night prior to the exam. I usually set aside some time before an exam to sip on some coffee (decaf) and read a book. Often, I would read my Bible and remind myself that my GPA does not determine who I am. Sometimes, I would just enjoy a great science fiction novel and let my imagination run. This usually gave me an extra boost and allowed my body and mind to relax.

### 2) Get 7-8 hours of uninterrupted sleep the night before.

On the 4.0 plan, you are guaranteed 8 hours of sleep, even on the night before an exam. So many horror stories about disastrous test performances start with the students doing an all-nighter the night before a critical exam. Would you trust someone to drive your brand new car when he or she was sleep deprived and delirious? Of course not! Walking into an exam half-asleep and physically exhausted is a sure-fire recipe for disaster.

### 3) Stay ON-PLAN!

When you are confident in your understanding of the class material, your stress level and test anxiety automatically reduces. The Guaranteed 4.0 plan makes it easy for you to remember the material. When you are on-plan, course materials are stored in your long-term memory by repetitious review of BPR, BPN, and BPC. In short, staying on-plan is your best defense against test anxiety. Before the exam, simply review your BPR, BPN and BPC to reinforce your learning. If it is a problem-based exam such as physics or math, do some practice problems to increase speed and accuracy. This will further increase your confidence as well.

✦ ✦ ✦ ✦ ✦ ✦ ✦ ✦ ✦

### *Dealing with Test Anxiety*

1. **Enjoy your weekly stress relieving / preventing activity**
2. **Get 7-8 hours of uninterrupted sleep the night before**
3. **Stay On-PLAN!**

✦ ✦ ✦ ✦ ✦ ✦ ✦ ✦ ✦

## FAQ #12  What are some test-taking strategies BEFORE the exam?

### 1) Pack your bag the night before.

Nothing is worse than walking into an exam only to realize that you forgot the calculator needed to complete the exam. I have personally witnessed a case in which a student walked into a civil engineering exam without a calculator; as a result, she had to wait for another student to finish before she could borrow the calculator. This is unnecessary drama that could easily be avoided by preparing your book bag the night before the exam with all of the necessary tools. This way, you won't forget what you need even if you are in a rush.

### 2) Avoid pre-exam chatters.

When a student arrives early for an exam and starts talking to his anxious classmates (pre-exam chatters), his anxiety level can easily be increased and his confidence can easily be destroyed. He could actually perform poorly despite the fact that he is well prepared for the test. To avoid this, simply get to class 5 minutes prior to the exam and do not engage in any pre-exam chatter. (Some students put on their headphones and listen to music until the instructor walks into the room with the exam.) Refuse to allow any negative or defeating thoughts into your head! Other students may feel the need to complain and be nervous, but not you. You are ON-PLAN and more than adequately prepared for the exam because the information is stored in your long-term memory!

✦ ✦ ✦ ✦ ✦ ✦ ✦ ✦ ✦

## *Prior to the Exam*

### 1. Pack your bag the night before.
### 2. Avoid pre-exam chatters.

✦ ✦ ✦ ✦ ✦ ✦ ✦ ✦ ✦

## FAQ #13  What are some test-taking strategies DURING the exam?

### 1) Check all instructions FIRST.

We all know the importance of paying attention to both verbal and written instructions. Unfortunately however, students often tend to jump into exams and immediately start to answer questions. A friend of mine received a lower grade in an architecture history class because he answered all three essay questions when the professor only required him to answer two. Because he had to allow time to write three essays, he did not have time to develop any of his answers fully. As soon as you get the test, take a minute to look through the instructions to know what is required of you.

### 2) Preview exam questions.

We suggest that you preview the exam questions. As you preview, BPs will start pouring into your brain because the material is stored in your long-term memory. If time allows, you can quickly write down BPs on a sheet of scratch paper or the margin of the exam paper. Once this process is finished, you are well on your way to successfully completing your exam. **Do not worry if you don't know how to approach a question.** Answer the problems that you can do first. As you work through the exam, additional BPs will be triggered that will probably help you answer the other questions.

### Example for Problem-based Exams

A problem on a chemistry exam reads:

> **Suppose you have a gas with a 45.0 ml volume and a pressure of 760 mmHg. If the pressure is increased to 800mmHg and the temperature remains constant, what is the new volume?**

As you preview, here are some BPs that may have been triggered.

- T = constant → Boyle's law
  - $P_1V_1 = P_2V_2$

Now, you have the equation to solve the problem and you can preview the next question.

### Example for Essay-based Exams

The paragraph in the essay exam reads:

> **Define and explain the third step of the Guaranteed 4.0**
> **Learning System in the order in which it was presented.**

As you preview the question, here are some BPs that may have come into your mind.

- **Define & Explain → 3rd step**
  - **IN ORDER**

- **3. Do what supposed to do**
  - **When supposed to do it**
    **BPR**
    **Class**
    **BPN**
    **HW**
    **POH**
    **BPC**
    **BP notebook**

By doing BPs while previewing, you now have the general structure of the essay. You can continue to develop the outline by adding more BPs and then converting all BPs into sentences for your essay.

Notice that doing BPs helps you to make sure that all relevant issues are addressed: the essay has to be explained "in order." Missing important essay keywords such as "contrast" or "define and give an example" can really put a damper on your grades.

### 3) Finish the exam with confidence.

I suggest bringing a watch or a small clock into the exam to help you keep track of the time. (If you use the cell phone clock, make sure it is on silent!) All that is left for you to do is to complete the exam with confidence. You can be confident because:

1. The material is in your long-term memory.
2. You have previewed the exam questions.
3. BPs give you a strategy for answering the questions.

❖ ❖ ❖ ❖ ❖ ❖ ❖ ❖ ❖ ❖

## *During the Exam*
### 1. CHECK all instructions FIRST
### 2. Preview all exam questions
###   • Write BPs as you preview
### 3. Finish the exam with confidence

❖ ❖ ❖ ❖ ❖ ❖ ❖ ❖ ❖ ❖

## FAQ #14 What are some test-taking strategies AFTER the exam?

### 1) Don't compare answers.

We all know the familiar scene: students huddle together after the exam and compare answers. To be honest, there are times my curiosity got the best of me and I compared answers with my classmates. I soon realized however that it was a lose-lose situation. Even when my answer matched that of a classmate, there was still a nagging possibility that we BOTH HAD IT WRONG! If my answer did not match, I spent the next couple of days consumed by stress! I learned my lesson the hard way!

In reality, comparing answers after an exam is both unproductive and stress inducing! It is unproductive because without going to the source (professor), you never really know if your answers are correct. Your time is not being used productively. It is stress inducing because the test is over and there is really nothing you can do about it. If your classmates want to compare answers with you after a test, just politely let them know that you are happy that the test is over and that you want to move on to your next task.

### 2) BPC returned exams.

### 3) POH

Since the benefits of doing BPC and utilizing POH have been explained in previous chapters, I won't belabor the point here. I will however share a real story with you that I believe will solidify the benefits in your mind. I took a tough civil engineering class during my junior year. I made a low B on the midterm while half of my classmates failed the exam! As a student on the 4.0 plan, I was somewhat discouraged. Nevertheless, I stayed on plan by continuing to do my BPCs and utilizing POH to receive additional understanding.

Two weeks later, the professor scheduled a make-up test that would replace our midterm grade if we made a higher score. The professor actually gave us the exact same test that we took at midterm! Armed with knowledge from BPC and POH, I aced that exam! However, much to my professor's dismay, the majority of my classmates (who were not ON PLAN) did not improve their grades and some even had lower scores!

✦ ✦ ✦ ✦ ✦ ✦ ✦ ✦ ✦ ✦

## *After the Exam*

### 1. Don't compare answers
### 2. BPC returned exams
### 3. POH

✦ ✦ ✦ ✦ ✦ ✦ ✦ ✦ ✦ ✦

### FAQ #15  How do I make my bed in 3 seconds or less?

Let's face it, making up your bed every morning is a chore that is enjoyed by few. For some of us, our beds are in a permanent state of disarray with the bed sheets, comforter, pillows and some school-related papers all in one gigantic clump. The good news is, it doesn't have to be this way any-more! As promised in Part 1 of the book, I will show you how to make your bed so that it only takes three seconds or less to remake it each morn-ing. You don't even have to sleep on top of the comforter!

This technique is referred to as "hospital corners" or "military corners." Here are the steps toward making a perfect "corner":

1) Put a fitted sheet on your mattress first.

2) Place the flat sheet on the bed. Tuck it in at the end of the bed where your feet will be. Do not tuck the sides!

3) On one side, about 1 foot from the end of the bed, lift the bottom of the hanging sheet and place it on the bed. Lift it up so it makes a diagonal fold (about a 45 degree angle).

4) Take the part of the sheet that is still hanging in that spot and tuck it under the mattress. Drop

the fold and pull it until the sheet is smooth. This creates a double-tuck. Do the same procedure on the other side.

5) Simply pull the flat sheet to cover the rest of the bed. The flat sheet can be folded down at the top. If you use a blanket, do the corners the same way. Now add a comforter. Put a pillow on top of the bed, and you are done.

Because the flat sheet is folded in a double tuck, it won't get pulled off of the bed when you toss and turn at night (no matter how badly you sleep). In the morning, all you have to do is straighten out the top sheet, pull up your comforter or blanket and reposition your pillows or other cute stuffed animals (if you have any). That generally takes only 3 seconds. Now you can have a cleaner room in just 3 seconds every morning!

### FAQ #16  How do I keep my room clean?

The objective here is to never let your room get dirty. As Donna O. mentioned, there are 3 main reasons that your room could be dirty. Since we already discussed the express "bed-making" techniques in FAQ #15, we will concentrate on dealing with piles of clothes (dirty or clean) and papers in your room.

To get rid of piles of clothes: purchase 2 upright rectangular hampers with lids. (They can be easily found in your neighborhood Wal-Mart or Target and cost about $5 each.) Use one hamper to store light-colored laundry and the other one for dark-colored clothes. When you get undressed, immediately place the dirty laundry into its "rightful resting place." **By doing this, the piles of clothes are eliminated, and your laundry is already separated.** If you plan to wear something again, (college students generally wear the same jeans at least 3 times as a rule of thumb!), go ahead and hang it up. It only takes 5 seconds to hang up a pair of jeans. It takes about 10 seconds to justify adding it to your ever-growing pile of clothes!

To deal with piles of papers in your room: you need a convenient desktop file organizer and some file folders. Create an individual file for things that you use frequently. For example, if you are addicted to ordering out to escape the dreadful cafeteria food, you should create a file labeled "TAKEOUTS" to

store menus and "buy 1 get 1 free" coupons from your favorite pizza place. Other possible file categories could include:

Current Bills
(Example: this month's phone bill, etc.)

Organizations
(Example: flyers and meeting notes, etc.)

Important documents
(Example: class schedule, tuition payment receipts, etc.)

Banking Statements
(Example: bank and credit card statements, etc.)

Paid Bills / Statements
(Example: previous cell phone bills, etc.)

Having a clean room is easier than you think. **The principle is this: everything has a place and everything is in its place.** You will be able to find things quickly and avoid disorderly surroundings that can hinder your grades.

## FAQ #17  How do I manage my time on the Guaranteed 4.0 plan?

The third step of the Guaranteed 3 Steps is "Do what you are supposed to do when you are supposed to do it." By creating a schedule that plots out the course of events for your entire week, you no longer have to wonder, "What am I supposed to be doing now?" We will take you through filling out your own schedule step by step. From now on, you should refer to your schedule as your "Plan for Success"!

## Step 1: How much time do you need in a week?

Using the What You Do in a Week table below, add up the time that it takes you to accomplish everything you need to in a week.

Remember, ✸ indicates a non-negotiable activity.

## Table: What You Do in a Week

| | Activity | Personal Estimate (Hours/Week) |
|---|---|---|
| ✺ | Class (Actual # of hours in the classroom) | |
| ✺ | Lab (Actual # of hours in lab) | |
| ✺ | BPR, BPN, HW, POH, BPC (Class x 1.5 + lab write-up time) | |
| ✺ | Sleep | |
| ✺ | Personal Hygiene (PH) | |
| ✺ | Relax / Planning | |
| (✺) | Church / Worship | |
| | Work | |
| | Eat | |
| | Extra-curricular Activities | |
| | Social | |
| | Exercise | |
| | Laundry / Cleaning | |
| | Errands | |
| | Transportation | |
| | **Total Needed (No more than 168 hours)** | |

## Step 2: Schedule Non-negotiable items

In Step 2, begin filling out your weekly schedule. You will find blank schedules that are included with the book. You can also set up an Excel spreadsheet and prepare your schedule that way. We have also enclosed two sample schedules and blank forms for your reference in the Appendix.

A. **Pencil in the exact time for each of your classes and labs.**
   - Use the subject name, such as English or Eng 300. **Do not** write "class."
   - Include the time it takes to get to and from class here. **Remember: you want to be in class 5 minutes early.**

B. **Determine a realistic time that you need to get up and prepare for class**.
   - Calculate the time that you need to go to bed the previous night in order to get the optimal amount of uninterrupted sleep (8 hours for most people).
   - By realistic we mean don't schedule yourself to get up at 5:30 AM if you are currently sleeping until 9:00 AM.

C. **Plan time for Personal Hygiene (PH)**.
   - You know what you need to do.

D. **Schedule your Bullet Point Notes (BPNs) as soon as possible after each class**.
   - Write it as BPN-Class Name. For example: BPN-Eng.
   - Plan 10 to 15 minutes for BPNs for each hour of class.
   - If you have two classes back to back, BPN both classes immediately after the second class.
   - If you have 3 or more classes back to back, you may want to plan a **short** break before doing your BPNs.

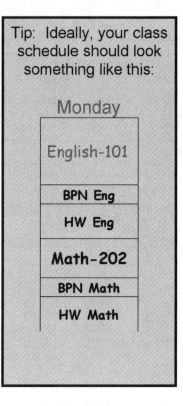

Tip: Ideally, your class schedule should look something like this:

Monday

English-101

BPN Eng

HW Eng

Math-202

BPN Math

HW Math

E. **Write in each of your Professor's Office Hours (POH)**.
   - Write it as POH-Class Name. For example: POH-Math.
   - Plan to spend approximately 15 to 20 minutes for each POH.
   - If there are multiple POH being offered, schedule POH before your weekly HW due date. That way, you can always ask questions about the HW.

F. **Schedule Homework (HW)**.
   - Write it as HW-Class Name. For example: HW Eng-101.
   - Start all HW the day it is assigned. Do HW problems from each section covered in lecture that day.
   - You do not necessarily need to finish it that day.

G. **Schedule Bullet Point Reading (BPR).**
   - Write it as BPR-Class Name. For example: BPR-History. For many liberal arts classes, your assigned HW is reading the class material. You can write it in as HW/BPR – Class Name. For example, HW/BPR- History.
   - Schedule your BPR at least **1-7 days before class**. You may choose to read for each lecture individually or for the entire week.
   - Here is a short cut to scheduling BPR that keeps it consistent throughout the week.
       - Monday → BPR for this Wednesday's classes.
       - Tuesday → BPR for this Thursday's classes.
       - Wednesday → BPR for this Friday's classes
       - Thursday → BPR for next Tuesday's classes.
       - Friday or Weekend → BPR for next Monday's classes.

H. **Schedule Bullet Point Concepts (BPC).**
   - Write it as BPC-Class Name. For example: BPC-Math.
   - BPCs can be scheduled the day HW is returned or once a week for all classes.
   - BPCs normally require 10 to 15 minutes for a standard HW set.

I. **Set aside time for planning.**
   - Take 15 to 30 minutes per week to schedule negotiable activities.

J. **Take time to relax.**
   - Schedule breaks each day.
   - Allow 1 to 2 hours a week for your stress relieving / preventing activity.

K. **Schedule time for Church / Worship**
   - For those who attend, this is considered a non-negotiable activity because you can't call your pastor or leader and ask him to reschedule service for you.

L. **Highlight all non-negotiable items on your schedule**
   - This is the only use you will have for your highlighter under the Guaranteed 4.0 plan.

## Step 3: Schedule Negotiable Items

Negotiable items are those that can be moved around or skipped entirely if necessary in your pursuit of a 4.0 GPA. However, be diligent to schedule these realistically. Negotiable items can fit into any of the blank spaces still existing on the schedule.

M. **Schedule work hours (your second job) if necessary.**
- Work is typically considered nego-tiable because
    1. Your work schedule can often be changed to fit your new 4.0 schedule,
    2. If you need to spend time doing BPR, BPN, HW, POH and BPC, work can often be rescheduled or shortened temporarily
    3. Most employers allow students to work flexible hours.

N. **Schedule other negotiable items. These can include:**
- Meals
- Exercise
- Laundry / Cleaning
- Paying bills
- Social time
- Extra-curricular
- Errands
- Hobbies
- Anything else...

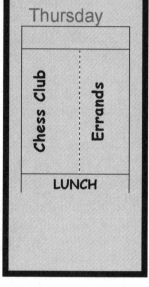

Tip: When filling in time slots that can be multi-tasked or that change each week, draw a dotted line down the center of the time slot and write in different activities on each side, like so:

## Step 4: Reality Check – "Keep it real!"

O. **Are you operating in reality?**
- Did you schedule BPR or HW on a Friday night?
- Are you trying to wake up more than an hour earlier than you currently are?

P. **Did you forget anything?**
- Use the following chart to determine if your schedule has all of the "bare necessities" for each class:

| Class: | Class: | Class: | Class: | Class: |
|--------|--------|--------|--------|--------|
| ❑ BPR<br>❑ CLASS<br>❑ BPN<br>❑ HW<br>❑ POH<br>❑ BPC | ❑ BPR<br>❑ CLASS<br>❑ BPN<br>❑ HW<br>❑ POH<br>❑ BPC | ❑ BPR<br>❑ CLASS<br>❑ BPN<br>❑ HW<br>❑ POH<br>❑ BPC | ❑ BPR<br>❑ CLASS<br>❑ BPN<br>❑ HW<br>❑ POH<br>❑ BPC | ❑ BPR<br>❑ CLASS<br>❑ BPN<br>❑ HW<br>❑ POH<br>❑ BPC |

## FAQ #18  How do I catch up without falling behind?

Let's just say that you began the Guaranteed 4.0 Plan after the beginning of your current semester. You want to stay on plan, but you already have a backlog of reading and homework. We will teach you how to get caught up without falling behind by showing you how to take advantage of the "negotiable" time in your schedule.

In short, we will quickly walk you through the process of identifying those tasks that need to be performed (using your new terminology: BPR, BPN, BPC, HW) and deciding when to do them. The secret to not getting further behind is in sticking with your non-negotiable activities as illustrated in your schedule.

By doing this, most students get caught up within a week. Of course, this all depends on how much you want to sacrifice in terms of negotiable activities, such as errands or social time. There will be a cost, but there will also be great benefits!

**Preparation: At this point, you should have already completed the weekly schedule. If not, see FAQ #17 for detailed instructions! DO NOT attempt to do the following exercise without first finishing your 4.0 "Plan for Success"!**

## STEP ONE: Breaking it Down

Now you will separate your backlog of work using your new "On Plan" terms. List one chapter of BPR or one HW assignment or one week of BPNs or one Exam/HW worth of BPCs that you need to catch up with on each blank line. For example, if you need to BPR and HW chapters 4 and 5 in English 300 along with BPN and BPC for Math 202, put these tasks on separate lines.

**EXAMPLE**

It is very important to list individual activities or assignments.

### "Catching up without falling behind" Planner - Page 1

| Class | Activity | Chapter or Assignment | ... | ... | ... |
|---|---|---|---|---|---|
| Eng 300 | BPR | Chap 4 | | | |
| Eng 300 | BPR | Chap 5 | | | |
| Eng 300 | HW | Chap 4 | | | |
| Eng 300 | HW | Chap 5 | | | |
| Math 202 | BPN | Week 6 | | | |
| Math 202 | BPN | Week 7 | | | |
| Math 202 | BPC | Quiz #2 | | | |
| Math 202 | BPC | Midterm | | | |

Notice:

- You do not need to do BPR for all missed reading if you are drastically behind, unless you know for a fact that you need details from the text.

- Blank 4.0 planner pages can be found in the Appendix

## STEP TWO: Estimating Time

For each line entered, estimate the amount of time you feel it will take you to complete the task. For instance, you may decide that it will take you one hour to BPR Chapter 4 for your English class. Write this in the column, **Estimated Time**.

| Class | Activity | Chapter or Assignment | Estimated Time | ... | ... |
|-------|----------|-----------------------|----------------|-----|-----|
| Eng 300 | BPR | Chap 4 | 1 Hour | | |
| Eng 300 | BPR | Chap 5 | 1 Hour | | |
| Eng 300 | HW | Chap 4 | 1.5 Hour | | |
| Eng 300 | HW | Chap 5 | 1.5 Hour | | |
| Math 202 | BPN | Week 6 | 15 Min. | | |
| Math 202 | BPN | Week 7 | 15 Min. | | |
| Math 202 | BPC | Quiz #2 | 30 Min. | | |
| Math 202 | BPC | Midterm | 45 Min. | | |

## STEP THREE: "Keeping it REAL!"

Determine your own personal **Human Factor**. This is the amount of time you need to add to your estimation to get closer to reality. If projects tend to take you longer than you anticipate, you may have a Human Factor of 30 minutes or even more. If you always complete your projects in the amount of time you estimate, you can use a Human Factor of 0 minutes. Write the number in the **Human Factor** column.

| Class | Activity | Chapter or Assignment | Estimated Time | Human Factor | ... |
|-------|----------|-----------------------|----------------|--------------|-----|
| Eng 300 | BPR | Chap 4 | 1 Hour | 30 Min. | |
| Eng 300 | BPR | Chap 5 | 1 Hour | 30 Min. | |
| Eng 300 | HW | Chap 4 | 1.5 Hour | 0 Min. | |
| Eng 300 | HW | Chap 5 | 1.5 Hour | 0 Min. | |
| Math 202 | BPN | Week 6 | 15 Min. | 0 Min. | |
| Math 202 | BPN | Week 7 | 15 Min. | 0 Min. | |
| Math 202 | BPC | Quiz #2 | 30 Min. | 0 Min. | |
| Math 202 | BPC | Midterm | 45 Min. | 15 Min. | |

## STEP FOUR: Final Calculation

On each line, **add the Human Factor to the Estimated Time to get the Final Calculation.** This is the amount of time you will need to allocate to complete the assignment on that line.

| Class | Activity | Chapter or Assignment | Estimated Time | Human Factor | Final Calculation |
|-------|----------|----------------------|----------------|--------------|-------------------|
| Eng 300 | BPR | Chap 4 | 1 Hour | 30 Min. | 1.5 Hour |
| Eng 300 | BPR | Chap 5 | 1 Hour | 30 Min. | 1.5 Hour |
| Eng 300 | HW | Chap 4 | 1.5 Hour | 0 Min. | 1.5 Hour |
| Eng 300 | HW | Chap 5 | 1.5 Hour | 0 Min. | 1.5 Hour |
| Math 202 | BPN | Week 6 | 15 Min. | 0 Min. | 15 Min. |
| Math 202 | BPN | Week 7 | 15 Min. | 0 Min. | 15 Min. |
| Math 202 | BPC | Quiz #2 | 30 Min. | 0 Min. | 45 Min. |
| Math 202 | BPC | Midterm | 45 Min. | 15 Min. | 1 Hour |
| | | | | **TOTAL** | **8 Hrs 15 Min** |

Now, prioritize the items in your table based on the degree of difficulty and deadline. Hint, place priority on the items you perceive to be more difficult.

## STEP FIVE: "Working it out!"

Now let's re-work your weekly schedule. **Be sure not to change any of your highlighted Non-Negotiable items.** These are the tasks that you must complete in order to not get further behind.

In the negotiable time slots of your schedule, find activities that you can temporarily give up until you are successfully caught up. Because you did not get behind in one day, **don't try to get caught up in one day and fall prey to the mentality of "THIS WEEKEND, I will get caught up" myth!** It is mentally overwhelming if you attempt to complete the entire 8.25 hours in one day. Instead, you should look for 1 - 2 hour openings on your schedule over multiple days. Activities are individually estimated so they can be easily "plugged" into the negotiable time slots on your schedule.

Use your discretion in deciding what you need to give up, but keep it real. Items that make good candidates are: social time, errands, and extra-curricular activities. Find and replace negotiable time in your week with catch-up activities from your table. If you simply cannot find enough time in a week (which is rare), you will need to stretch your catch-up period to two weeks. Follow your new schedule until you are caught up with the 4.0 plan. Make adjustments to the schedule as necessary.

**Write down your plan of action** using the "Catching up without falling behind" Planner. Psychologically, you will be more committed to the plan if you write it down clearly and post the plan somewhere visible.

### Example of the Guaranteed 4.0
### "Catching up without falling behind" Planner - Page 2

| Date | List of Activities | Time | Accomplished? |
|------|--------------------|------|----------------|
| Monday | BPR- Eng Ch. 4 | 3–4:30 P.M. | Yes |
| Monday | BPN- Math – class 6 & 7 | 9:30–10 P.M. | Yes |
| Tuesday | HW- Eng Ch. 4 | 1–2:30 P.M. | |
| Wednesday | BPC- Math Quiz 2 | 5–5:45 P.M. | |
| Thursday | BPR- Eng Ch. 5 | 1–2:30 P.M. | |
| Thursday | BPC- Math Midterm | 6–7:00 P.M. | |
| Friday | HW – Eng Ch. 5 | 3–4:30 P.M. | |

As you can see from this example, this student wrote down a plan of action and had already accomplished Monday's tasks. As this student stays on this plan, she will be completely caught up by Friday at 4:30 pm. This will allow her to fully enjoy the weekend without the dark cloud of "I need to catch up" hanging over her head.

**Y.C.'s Confession time:**

Periodically, even the student with the best intentions can "fall off the wagon" and fall behind on the Guaranteed 4.0 Plan. I know this method works, because it got me "back on the wagon" a few times. (I guess it's too late to plead the Fifth!) In fact, the example you see above is a true "catching up without falling behind" plan because I was the student! This method is extremely effective, especially for someone like me who is not naturally organized.

### FAQ #19 I just learned the 4.0 plan and I have a test this week; what can I do?

In the ideal world, students will learn the Guaranteed 4.0 plan prior to the start of an academic term. However, this is not a perfect world. Many students often do not learn about the 4.0 plan until the middle or the latter part of the semester or quarter. If you fall in this category and you have a test coming up within a week (or even tomorrow), here is the "quick and dirty" method for getting ready for a test!

**First, do BPN on the class notes.** When you can understand and BP the important concepts covered in class, you have a good foundation in preparing for a test. When you BPN for problem-based classes (such as math and science), pay special attention to HOW the professor solved certain problems. This may give you an advantage on the test because you are gaining insight into the professor's thinking. (Many professors want to see problems solved their way for ease of grading.) By doing BPN, you are effectively reviewing in a productive fashion!

**Second, do BPC on corrected HW, quizzes or study guides (if applicable!)** BPC can help you get to the WHY behind the question, especially when your professor has graciously assigned HW or given a study guide on the material covered on the test. If you understand the principles and concepts covered in homework or previous quizzes, you will be better prepared to solve the problems on the upcoming exam.

**Third, use POH to get any questions answered and gain further insight from the professor on how to prepare.**

### FAQ #20 If I have questions after reading this book, who can help me?

**You can register for FREE to become part of our 4.0 web communities at www.Guaranteed4.com.** There are postings on discussion boards and you will get notification for our regularly scheduled chat room Q & A sessions. The site also has a webpage where you can send us an email with your questions. You can expect an answer within 48 hours. We are serious about your academic success and you are not alone in this process!

# Appendix

# Blank Charts
# and Examples

# Plan for Success

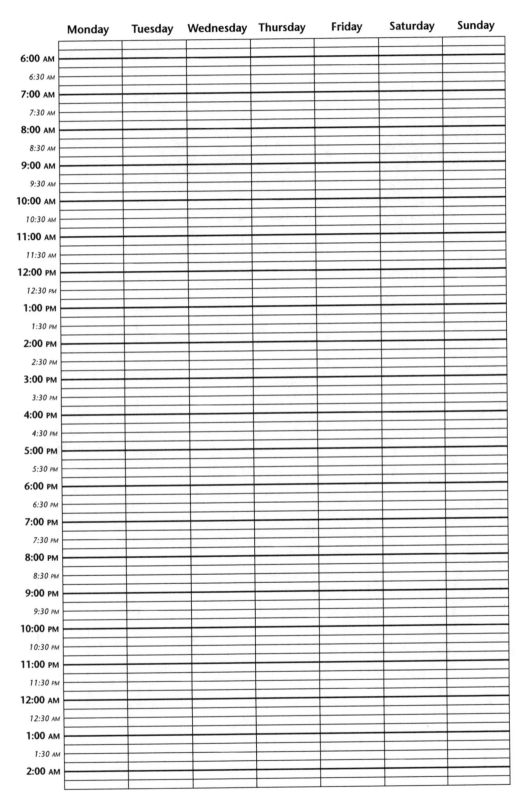

|  | Monday | Tuesday | Wednesday | Thursday | Friday | Saturday | Sunday |
|---|---|---|---|---|---|---|---|
| 6:00 AM | | | | | | | |
| 6:30 AM | | | | | | | |
| 7:00 AM | | | | | | | |
| 7:30 AM | | | | | | | |
| 8:00 AM | | | | | | | |
| 8:30 AM | | | | | | | |
| 9:00 AM | | | | | | | |
| 9:30 AM | | | | | | | |
| 10:00 AM | | | | | | | |
| 10:30 AM | | | | | | | |
| 11:00 AM | | | | | | | |
| 11:30 AM | | | | | | | |
| 12:00 PM | | | | | | | |
| 12:30 PM | | | | | | | |
| 1:00 PM | | | | | | | |
| 1:30 PM | | | | | | | |
| 2:00 PM | | | | | | | |
| 2:30 PM | | | | | | | |
| 3:00 PM | | | | | | | |
| 3:30 PM | | | | | | | |
| 4:00 PM | | | | | | | |
| 4:30 PM | | | | | | | |
| 5:00 PM | | | | | | | |
| 5:30 PM | | | | | | | |
| 6:00 PM | | | | | | | |
| 6:30 PM | | | | | | | |
| 7:00 PM | | | | | | | |
| 7:30 PM | | | | | | | |
| 8:00 PM | | | | | | | |
| 8:30 PM | | | | | | | |
| 9:00 PM | | | | | | | |
| 9:30 PM | | | | | | | |
| 10:00 PM | | | | | | | |
| 10:30 PM | | | | | | | |
| 11:00 PM | | | | | | | |
| 11:30 PM | | | | | | | |
| 12:00 AM | | | | | | | |
| 12:30 AM | | | | | | | |
| 1:00 AM | | | | | | | |
| 1:30 AM | | | | | | | |
| 2:00 AM | | | | | | | |

# Plan for Success – Example A

| Time | Mon | Tue | Wed | Thu | Fri | Sat | Sun |
|---|---|---|---|---|---|---|---|
| 7:45-8:00 | P.H. | P.H. | P.H. | P.H. | P.H. | sleep | sleep |
| 8:00-15 | | | | | | ↓ | ↓ |
| 8:15-30 | Food | Food | Food | Food | Food | | |
| 8:30-45 | | | | | | | P.H. |
| 8:45-9:00 | Trans. | Trans. | Trans. | Trans. | Trans. | | Food |
| 9:00-15 | English | History | English | History | English | | |
| 9:15-30 | | | | | | | |
| 9:30-45 | ↓ | | | | | ↓ | |
| 9:45-10:00 | | | | | | | Trans. |
| 10:00-15 | bpn - Eng | | bpn - Eng | | bpn - Eng | P.H. | Church |
| 10:15-30 | hw - Eng | ↓ | hw - Eng | ↓ | hw - Eng | | |
| 10:30-45 | | bpn - Hist. | | bpn - Hist. | | Food | |
| 10:45-11:00 | Trans. | Trans. | Trans. | Trans. | Trans. | | |
| 11:00-15 | Calc 1 | Calc 1 | Calc 1 | Calc 1 | Calc 1 | laundry | |
| 11:15-30 | | | | (Discussion) | | and | |
| 11:30-45 | | | | | | Clean | |
| 11:45-12:00 | ↓ | ↓ | ↓ | | ↓ | ↓ | ↓ |
| 12:00-15 | bpn-Calc | bpn-Calc | bpn-Calc | bpc-Calc | bpn-Calc | | social |
| 12:15-30 | Hw - Calc | Hw - Calc | Hw - Calc | Hw - Calc | Hw - Calc | | |
| 12:30-45 | | | | | | Extra- | ↓ |
| 12:45-1:00 | Lunch | Lunch | Lunch | Lunch | Lunch | Curr. | |
| 1:00-15 | | | | | | | Trans. |
| 1:15-30 | POH-Eng | social | POH-Calc | social | POH-Phy | | |
| 1:30-45 | | | | | | social | |
| 1:45-2:00 | Trans. | Trans. | Hw - Calc | Trans. | Trans. | | Errands |
| 2:00-15 | Physics | Physics | | Physics | Hw - Calc | | |
| 2:15-30 | LAB | | Trans. | | | | |
| 2:30-45 | | | POH-Hist | | break | | |
| 2:45-3:00 | | | | | bpr - eng | | |
| 3:00-15 | | | Errands | | | | bpr - phy |
| 3:15-30 | | | | | | | |
| 3:30-45 | ↓ | bpn - phy. | | bpn - phy. | | | |
| 3:45-4:00 | | Hw - phy | | Hw - phy | Errands | Exercise | |
| 4:00-15 | bpn - p.lab | | bpr - Hist. | | | | break |
| 4:15-30 | Hw - p.lab | | | | Extra- | | Hw - p.lab |
| 4:30-45 | | | | | Curr. | | |
| 4:45-5:00 | Errands | break | | Errands | | ↓ | bpc -hist. |
| 5:00-15 | Exercise | bpc -phy | break | | | P.H. | break |
| 5:15-30 | | | bpc -phy | POH-phy | Exercise | | bpr - eng |
| 5:30-45 | | Hw - Calc | | (lab) | | social | |
| 5:45-6:00 | ↓ | | bpr - phy | Hw - Hist. | | | |
| 6:00-15 | P.H. | Food | | | | | Food |
| 6:15-30 | | | | | | | |
| 6:30-45 | | social | | | | | ↓ |
| 6:45-7:00 | Food | | Food | Food | P.H. | | |
| 7:00-15 | | Hw - Hist. | | | | | break |
| 7:15-30 | Hw - Calc | | social | social | Food | | bpr - calc |
| 7:30-45 | | | | | | | |
| 7:45-8:00 | social | | bpr - calc | bpc -eng | social | | ↓ |
| 8:00-15 | | Extra- | | | | | bpr - Hist. |
| 8:15-30 | ↓ | Curr. | ↓ | Trans. | | | |
| 8:30-45 | | | | Extra- | | | |
| 8:45-9:00 | | | social | Curr. | | | |
| 9:00-15 | | | | | | | |
| 9:15-30 | | | | | | | |
| 9:30-45 | ↓ | social | ↓ | ↓ | | ↓ | planning |
| 9:45-10:00 | | | | | | | |
| 10:00-15 | | | | Trans. | | | ↓ |
| 10:15-30 | Relax | Relax | Relax | Relax | | | Relax |
| 10:30-45 | | | | | | | |
| 10:45-11:00 | | | | | ??? | | |
| 11:00-15 | ↓ | ↓ | ↓ | ↓ | | ↓ | ↓ |
| 11:15-30 | P.H. | P.H. | P.H. | P.H. | | P.H. | P.H. |
| 11:30-45 | | | | | | | |
| 11:45-12:00 | | | | | | | |

# Plan for Success – Example B

| Time | Mon | Tue | Wed | Thu | Fri | Sat | Sun |
|---|---|---|---|---|---|---|---|
| 7:45-8:00 | P.H. | P.H. | P.H. | P.H. | P.H. | sleep | sleep |
| 8:00-15 | | | | | | ↓ | ↓ |
| 8:15-30 | Food | Food | Food | Food | Food | | |
| 8:30-45 | | | | | | | P.H. |
| 8:45-9:00 | trans. | trans. | trans. | trans. | trans. | | |
| 9:00-15 | English | History | English | History | English | | Food |
| 9:15-30 | ↓ | ↓ | ↓ | ↓ | ↓ | ↓ | |
| 9:30-45 | | | | | | | Trans. |
| 9:45-10:00 | | | | | | P.H. | |
| 10:00-15 | bpn - Eng | | bpn - Eng | | bpn - Eng | | Church |
| 10:15-30 | hw - Eng | | hw - Eng | | hw - Eng | Food | |
| 10:30-45 | | bpn - Hist. | | bpn - Hist. | | | |
| 10:45-11:00 | Trans. | Trans. | Trans. | Trans. | Trans. | laundry and Clean | |
| 11:00-15 | Calc 1 | Calc 1 | Calc 1 | Calc 1 | Calc 1 | | |
| 11:15-30 | ↓ | ↓ | ↓ | ↓ | ↓ | | |
| 11:30-45 | | | | | | ↓ | ↓ |
| 11:45-12:00 | | | | | | | social |
| 12:00-15 | bpn-Calc | bpn-Calc | bpn-Calc | bpn-Calc | bpn-Calc | | |
| 12:15-30 | Hw - Calc | Hw - Calc | Hw - Calc | Hw - Calc | Hw - Calc | | ↓ |
| 12:30-45 | | | | | | Extra-Curr. | |
| 12:45-1:00 | Lunch | Lunch | Lunch | Lunch | Lunch | | Trans. |
| 1:00-15 | | | | | | | |
| 1:15-30 | POH-Eng | social | POH-Calc | social | POH-phy | social | Errands |
| 1:30-45 | | | | | | | |
| 1:45-2:00 | Trans. | Trans. | Trans. | Trans. | Trans. | | |
| 2:00-15 | Physics LAB | Physics | POH-Hist | Physics | Hw - Calc | | bpr - calc |
| 2:15-30 | | ↓ | | | | | ↓ |
| 2:30-45 | | | Hw - Calc | | break | | |
| 2:45-3:00 | | | | | bpr - Hist. | | |
| 3:00-15 | | | break | | | | break |
| 3:15-30 | | | bpr - Hist. | | | | bpr - phy |
| 3:30-45 | | bpn - phy. | | bpn - phy. | | | |
| 3:45-4:00 | ↓ | Hw - phy | ↓ | Hw - phy | Extra-Curr. | | ↓ |
| 4:00-15 | bpn - p.lab | | | | | | break |
| 4:15-30 | Hw - p.lab | ↓ | Extra-Curr. | ↓ | | | Hw - p.lab |
| 4:30-45 | | | | | | | |
| 4:45-5:00 | Errands | break | | Errands | Errands | | bpc -calc |
| 5:00-15 | | bpc -phy | Exercise | POH-phy (lab) | Exercise | | |
| 5:15-30 | Exercise | | | | | | bpc -hist. |
| 5:30-45 | | Hw - Calc | | Hw - Hist. | | | |
| 5:45-6:00 | | | | | | | |
| 6:00-15 | ↓ | Food | ↓ | ↓ | ↓ | | Relax |
| 6:15-30 | | | | | | | |
| 6:30-45 | | social | | | | | ↓ |
| 6:45-7:00 | P.H. | | P.H. | Food | P.H. | | |
| 7:00-15 | | Hw - Hist. | | | | | Planning |
| 7:15-30 | Food | | Food | social | Food | | |
| 7:30-45 | | ↓ | | | | | ↓ |
| 7:45-8:00 | social | | social | Hw - Calc | social | | |
| 8:00-15 | | bpc -calc | | | | | social |
| 8:15-30 | Hw - Calc | | bpc -phy | bpc -eng | | | |
| 8:30-45 | | break | | | | | ↓ |
| 8:45-9:00 | bpr - eng | bpr - calc | bpr - phy | bpr - eng | ↓ | | |
| 9:00-15 | | | | | | | |
| 9:15-30 | ↓ | ↓ | ↓ | ↓ | | | ↓ |
| 9:30-45 | | | | | | | |
| 9:45-10:00 | Relax | Relax | Relax | Relax | | | Relax |
| 10:00-15 | | | | | | | |
| 10:15-30 | ↓ | ↓ | ↓ | ↓ | ??? | | ↓ |
| 10:30-45 | | | | | | | |
| 10:45-11:00 | P.H. | P.H. | P.H. | P.H. | | P.H. | P.H. |
| 11:00-15 | | | | | | | |

## *"Catching up without falling behind" Planner A - Page 1*

| Class | Activity | Chapter or Assignment | Estimated Time | Human Factor | Final Calculation |
|-------|----------|----------------------|----------------|--------------|-------------------|
|       |          |                      |                |              |                   |
|       |          |                      |                |              |                   |
|       |          |                      |                |              |                   |
|       |          |                      |                |              |                   |
|       |          |                      |                |              |                   |
|       |          |                      |                |              |                   |
|       |          |                      |                |              |                   |
|       |          |                      |                |              |                   |
|       |          |                      |                |              |                   |
|       |          |                      |                |              |                   |
|       |          |                      |                |              |                   |
|       |          |                      |                |              |                   |
|       |          |                      |                |              |                   |
|       |          |                      |                |              |                   |
|       |          |                      |                |              |                   |

# "Catching up without falling behind" Planner B - Page 2

| Date | List of Activities | Time | Accomplished? |
|------|-------------------|------|---------------|
|      |                   |      |               |
|      |                   |      |               |
|      |                   |      |               |
|      |                   |      |               |
|      |                   |      |               |
|      |                   |      |               |
|      |                   |      |               |
|      |                   |      |               |
|      |                   |      |               |
|      |                   |      |               |
|      |                   |      |               |
|      |                   |      |               |
|      |                   |      |               |
|      |                   |      |               |

## SEMINARS AND WORKSHOPS

Guaranteed 4.0 presenters are available to facilitate customized learning seminars and workshops for various types of audiences. For more information, please refer to our website at www.Guaranteed4.com or call 972.236.5673.

## WRITE TO US

It is our mission to positively impact the life of every student who reads this book or attends 4.0 seminars. When you experienced success in following the 4.0 Plan, we would love to hear from you. Please submit your testimonials via email to:

**Info@guaranteed4.com**
Re: testimonial

## ATTENTION: Civic, Professional & Educational Organizations

Quantity discounts are available on bulk purchases of this book for educational purposes, subscription / membership incentives, gifts, fundraising and reselling. Special books or book excepts can also be created to fit specific needs. For information, please email us at:

**sales@NoMoreStudy.com**
Re: Bulk Purchases

## Give the Gift of Extraordinary Learning
## To Your Love Ones, Friends and Colleagues

**Check our store at www.NoMoreStudy.com for current promotions**
or CHECK YOUR LEADING BOOKSTORE
or ORDER HERE

❏ **YES, I want _____ copies of Guaranteed 4.0** at $19.95 each, plus $ 4 shipping per shipping address (Texas residents please add $ 1.60 sales tax per book). All orders must be accompanied by a postal money order in U.S. Funds. Please allow 15 days for delivery.

❏ **My money order for $ ____ is enclosed for this order.**

❏ **Please charge my _____Visa or _____ MasterCard for this order.**

Name _____

Organization _____

Street Address _____

City / State / Zip _____

Phone _____ Email _____

Card # _____ Exp. Date _____

Signature _____

**Please make MONEY ORDER payable to and return the form to:**

Guaranteed 4.0 Learning System
17194 Preston Road, Suite 102 MC 338
Dallas, Texas 75248

**Please FAX your credit card order to: 972.236.5683**

Phone: 972.236.5673
sales@NoMoreStudy.com